work

@

home

"This well-researched and highly informative guide is for every woman with a heart for home."—Ginger Plowman, author of *Don't Make Me Count to Three* and *Heaven at Home*

"Whether you're seriously considering working from home or simply entertaining the idea, *Work@home* will help push away the fog and make the possibilities clear."—Sharon Jaynes, international speaker and author of more than ten books, including *Your Scars Are Beautiful to God* and *Becoming the Woman of His Dreams*

"If you are considering the possibility of working at home, need encouragement in your home business, or simply want help in managing your household, *Work@home* is the book you need."
—Mary Southerland, author, speaker, president of Journey Ministries

"This is the best book I've ever read on the subject of working from home. This is a must-have resource for anyone who is serious about working from home."—Sabrina O'Malone, president, WorkingMom.com

work
@
home

A Practical Guide

for Women Who

Want to Work

from Home

GLYNNIS WHITWER

NEW HOPE
P U B L I S H E R S

Birmingham, Alabama

New Hope® Publishers
P. O. Box 12065
Birmingham, AL 35202-2065
www.newhopepublishers.com

Library of Congress Cataloging-in-Publication Data
Whitwer, Glynnis, 1961-
  Work@home : a practical guide for women who want to work from
home /
Glynnis Whitwer.
     p. cm.
  ISBN-13: 978-1-59669-044-8 (soft cover)
  1. Work--Religious aspects--Christianity. 2. Home-based businesses.
3. Self-employed. 4. Home labor. 5. Telecommuting. 6. Work and
family. I. Title. II. Title: Work at home.
BT738.5.W53 2007
658'.0412082--dc22

                              2006026550

ISBN-10: 1-59669-044-5
ISBN-13: 978-1-59669-044-8

N074128 • 0307 • 3M1

CONTENTS . . . .

ACKNOWLEDGMENTS . . . .

It's an exciting, yet humbling experience to write a book. Exciting because . . . well . . . I've just written my first book!!! Humbling because I needed the help of so many people to actually do it. Thank you does not begin to express my gratitude to the following people I love and care so much about:

To my amazing husband, Tod. Not once did you doubt that I could do this. Thank you for the uncountable ways you supported me and loved me through this.

To my wonderful children, Joshua, Dylan, Robbie, Cathrine, and Ruth. You are precious gifts. Your love and faith in me is a shining light.

To my Writing Care Group at Vineyard North Phoenix. Thank you for your encouragement, prayer, and practical proofreading.

To my dear friends at Proverbs 31 Ministries. Thank you for shouldering my disappointments and now sharing in the joy of this book. Everyone should have such sweet spiritual sisters.

To my mom, Kathryn Owens. Thank you for making me believe I could conquer the world, for loving me unconditionally, and for dropping everything to proofread a chapter or iron some shirts.

To Julie Kuss. Thank you for seeing the potential in my writing, for helping fine-tune the message in this book, and for finding a publisher who caught the vision.

To Debra Cooper. Thank you for sharing your astute editing skills and making me a better writer.

To the team at New Hope Publishers. Thank you for believing that there's a need for this book and for making it happen. You are a beautiful group of believers and bring glory to God through your ministry at New Hope.

To Jesus Christ. Thank You for pouring out Your life so that mine has meaning. It's all about You.

CHAPTER 1

• • • • • • • •

UNDERSTANDING YOUR CALL

Most people who pick up a book like this want the bottom line. "Just tell me what I need to do to afford being home!" In fact, you may want to skip this chapter altogether and jump ahead to the budgeting pages.

But I would be doing you a disservice if I didn't start with the most important question of this entire book. Is God calling you to transition out of the workplace and be home?

You see, everyone has a different reason for wanting to be home.

- You may have children and long to spend more time with them. Perhaps you are tired of someone else spending the best part of the day with them. Maybe there's homeschooling in your future.
- Maybe you desire greater flexibility in your schedule and want to start your own business. Perhaps you hate your job. Each Sunday evening may begin a cycle of dread that keeps you awake that night and lasts for a good part of the week.

- Some of you are sick of having a dirty house. It's draining to spend all your free time at home just trying to keep up with the housework. Then, when the house is finally clean, you aren't there to enjoy it.
- Some husbands want their wives home, or vice versa, to have a nice dinner on the table every night and clean clothes ready.
- Some of you want to volunteer more hours at church or at your child's school. Maybe the Lord is calling you to a new ministry that isn't possible with full-time employment outside of the home.
- Some people need greater peace in their lives, and believe being home is the solution. Guess what? I hate to start off with bad news, but here's the truth. You can quit your job, transition home, and still none of your hopes can come true.
- You can put your kids in front of a TV and not invest more time in them.
- You can discover that starting a home-based business is more work than you ever imagined.
- You can hate being home alone all day.
- You can watch TV or go shopping and still have a dirty house.
- You can be disorganized without the structure of your previous job, and not plan meals or do laundry in a timely fashion.
- You can fill your days with tasks and not have any extra time to volunteer.
- You can actually have less peace because now you are around your kids all day, in a dirty house, with nothing in the fridge and a spouse who expects you to do it all since you're home.
- And if you haven't planned accordingly, you'll have the financial strain of being broke.

This is why it's critical to start the process by understanding your calling from God. If that's not in order, none of your hopes for staying home will come true. On the flip side, when you are confident in God's will, then your life will be filled with peace and joy despite the dirty dishes and crying kids.

Many people allow their lives to just flow like a river, without much thought being given to where they are going or where they would really like to go. Sometimes the water is smooth and gentle, yet at other times it's raging white water. We think, "I'll just take whatever this river of life brings."

My life reflected that attitude. Growing up I knew I would go to college, get married, have a career, and then have kids. For years I paddled down this course, accepting the current and bends in my personal river. I assumed I would always work in the corporate world. After all, I had a college degree and was on a path to success. I believed that since my closest friends worked and still managed a personal life, it could be done.

While that may be a good life for some, it wasn't God's best life for me.

Even though I accepted Christ as a young girl, never once did I think about asking God if He had any other plans for me. I was in the driver's seat and occasionally allowed God to peer over my shoulder from the backseat and offer a tip or two. His design for my life wasn't a top priority.

It took God crashing my boat on a rock to get me to consider another course. I didn't listen to God's gentle whispers when He told me to stay home and raise my children full-time. I continued to ignore Him as His voice became sterner when He told me to put my husband first. Finally, I believe He got fed up with my selective hearing and moved me 2,000 miles away from everything I knew and loved.

My pathway home wasn't filled with peace and joy. It was tinged with resentment over a move I didn't want and a change in my life I felt was forced upon me.

After I got over the sadness of moving, God began to reveal His plan for my life, which was to be home. Listening to God and obeying His plan has brought untold blessings to every member of my family.

My journey home is different from yours. You may long to be home. Your heart may break every time you drop your child at day care. You may have a family member experiencing an illness and need to be home. Your entrepreneurial spirit may long to start your own business from home. Perhaps you are nearing retirement and wondering how you will handle this transition.

Regardless of where you are in your transition home, now is the time to consider God's calling on your life, at this time, and commit yourself to His purpose for you.

God has a purpose for every person in this world. And He has uniquely equipped you for that purpose. Jeremiah 29:11 clearly shows that God knows you as an individual: "'For I know the plans I have for you,' declares the LORD, 'plans to prosper you and not to harm you, plans to give you hope and a future.'"

Perhaps you believe your life was an accident. Perhaps your parents didn't plan for you. My pastor says, "There are no illegitimate children—illegitimate parents maybe—but never children." God created you, you are His child, and He desires to have an intimate relationship with you. But, that involves you seeking His will and not your own.

Before making a major life change such as leaving the traditional workforce, it's critical to do some self-evaluation and determine if you are living according to your purpose for you or God's purpose for you. This is the first step in becoming the person God created you to be, and seeking His best at this time of your life.

In the remainder of this chapter we will discuss the following questions.

- Who am I?
- What is my purpose?
- Where am I to serve?

My hope is that by answering these questions, you will have a clearer sense of God's purpose for your life right now. This will either be a confirmation of your calling to transition home or a clarification of another direction.

WHO AM I?

Have you ever played the guessing game where someone tapes the name of a famous person on your back and then you have to ask yes or no questions to determine who you are?

Wouldn't life be easy if the answers about our God-given

identity were all printed out on a little card and handed to us when we reached age five?

Many of us live our lives trying to answer the question, Who am I? by what we do and how well we do it. We gauge our self-worth by how successful we are in our jobs, our marriage, with our children and our friends. We are confident in our value when circumstances are running smoothly.

But what happens when life gets rough? Self-worth built on accomplishments or relationships with others is a shaky foundation indeed.

God wants us to define our identity by His definition of us—no one else's. And His definition of us is wonderful. We are dearly beloved children of the King. The Scriptures are filled with beautiful pictures and stories of how beloved we are.

Many of us are on a quest for perfection. We dream of having the perfect life. We want the perfect spouse, the perfect house, and perfect children. I was personally enamored of being a professional businesswoman. I loved wearing suits and hearing the click clack of my high heels on the floor.

But fairly early on I knew my quest for perfection was hopeless.

I just never quite met my own standards. There was always a run in my hose or I'd forget an appointment. While others could mesmerize a crowd with dynamic words, I'd trip over my tongue trying to communicate a simple message. Everyone else drove cute cars without sliding doors.

In 2005, my husband and I adopted two little girls. For 14 years before that, I was the mother of three sons. I love being the mother of boys! But just once I wanted to simply walk through a mall—instead, we skipped, twirled, ran, and slid our way through most stores for many years.

One shopping trip when they were very small, I went shopping with a friend. She was trying on clothes and needed a smaller size. I had just delivered my third child and was trying to lose 30 pounds of "baby" weight. My friend, on the other hand, was looking for something smaller than a size 3.

I left my two older boys playing quietly with her daughter just outside the dressing room door while I stepped a few feet away to look for a smaller size. That in itself was enough to make me cringe when I asked the salesclerk for help (as if I had to explain it wasn't for me). But on the way back to the changing room I heard a very angry female voice yell, "Whose kids are these?"

It seemed my boys wanted to see what or who was in the next changing stall and surprised a woman in some stage of undress.

So, you can see how dangerous it would be if I based my self-worth and identity on my circumstances.

Here is the truth about who you are: You are a chosen child of God. You are loved so much that God sent His only Son to be the sacrifice for your sin, so that you might have intimate fellowship with Him eternally. The answer to this question, Who am I? is the foundation for your life.

I never thought I would have a problem answering this question. But when I left the workforce, I was floundering. I had based my answer to the question, Who am I? on what I did; and not only in the workforce, but at church. I left my job and church at the same time due to the move. When I no longer had anything to "perform," I doubted my worth.

Shortly after moving, I purchased a book called *No Ordinary Home* by Carol Brazo. I had determined to embrace my new role at home. Surprisingly, my questions about being a homemaker weren't answered in this book. Instead, the author led me to answer the question, Who am I?

She wrote, "If there were one biblical truth I wish I could give my children and lay hold of in my deepest parts, it would be this one thing. He created me, He loves me, He will always love me. Nothing I do will change who I am. Being versus doing. The error was finally outlined in bold. I was always worried about what I was doing. . . . God's only concern was and is what I am being—a child of His, forgiven, justified by the work of His Son, His heir."

His child . . . Paul tells us in Romans 8:16 that "the Spirit himself testifies with our spirit that we are God's children." We are—we don't have to earn that position.

When I read those words, I felt as if God spoke directly to me. I had been so concerned with doing the right things that I neglected to consider whether or not I was being the person God wanted me to be. God showed me He was far more concerned about my character than my performance.

This is a liberating truth and one that every Christian needs to grab hold of in his or her heart. If you have been trying to please God by something you are doing, then relax in His love. You can't make God love you any more or less by what you are doing.

WHAT IS MY PURPOSE?

The next logical question is, What is my purpose?

God designed everything to have a purpose. Now, I truly do wonder about cockroaches—but that's clearly my problem.

One of the first things God did after creating Adam was to assign him the job of taking care of Eden. In Genesis 2:15 we read, "The LORD God took the man and put him in the Garden of Eden to work it and take care of it." Adam had a purpose.

Knowing our purpose gives life meaning. I am a completely different person when I know my purpose. If I attend a conference or retreat as solely a participant, then I'm content to stay on the sidelines in my quiet corner. But if I have an assignment, such as registration or greeting, then everything takes on greater meaning.

In her book *Living Life on Purpose,* Lysa TerKeurst shares a powerful way to understand our purpose by using Romans 12:1–8 as a guide. First you declare your master; then you determine your mind-set; and, finally, you develop your makeup.

Declare your master.

"Therefore, I urge you, brothers, in view of God's mercy, to offer your bodies as living sacrifices, holy and pleasing to God—this is your spiritual act of worship" (Romans 12:1).

This Scripture verse calls us to voluntarily give our whole selves to God and to serve Him only. This is our primary purpose. When we declare that God is our master, we are surrendering our sinful natures to Him and our will for our lives. We are saying we will follow where He leads. We are standing up and proclaiming that we will serve the Lord.

This is a strong statement—it means no more riding the fence. You can't be a part-time Christian once you make this declaration.

Determine your mind-set.

"Do not conform any longer to the pattern of this world, but be transformed by the renewing of your mind. Then you will be able to test and approve what God's will is—His good, pleasing and perfect will" (Romans 12:2).

Christians are called to think differently. The world thinks about financial gain, being first in line, achieving more success, acquiring more goods—there's a focus on materialism and self-actualization. When we conform "to the pattern of this world," we make decisions based upon our own self-interests, what's best for me.

But God calls us to a different standard. When we renew our minds, when we choose to think about God's will, then He promises that our lives will be transformed. I don't know about you, but I need a transformation.

Don't look to the world for your purpose. You must know what the will of your master is if you are to accomplish your purpose. Look into God's Word and let your mind be transformed. Spend time in prayer, seeking God's will for you.

Describe and develop your makeup.

Once you have identified your master and determined your mind-set, you are ready to describe and develop your makeup.

For by the grace given me I say to every one of you: Do not think of yourself more highly than you ought, but rather think of yourself with sober judgment, in accordance with the measure of faith God has given you. Just as each of us has one body with many members, and these members do not all have the same function, so in Christ we who are many form one body, and each member belongs to all the others. We have different gifts, according to the grace given us (Romans 12:3–6).

God has handcrafted you and made you unique. Never before

or again will there be anyone like you. Your emotional, mental, and spiritual characteristics are distinctively you.

This Scripture passage indicates that each believer has different gifts and that each believer's purpose is to serve God and others. It is a beautiful picture of interdependence. In order to fulfill God's plan for His church here on earth, believers needs to know their gifts and then use them.

It's a human characteristic to want what others have. No place is this more true than in a restaurant. I can be confident that I want spaghetti and meatballs until I see my husband's lasagna.

I've often wished I had others' gifts and personal characteristics. I wish I were a better pray-er, a better counselor, and a better evangelist. I wish I were more outgoing, the life of the party, and carefree. But God has given me the gifts of administration and teaching, and I'm more reserved and cautious. God's plan is fulfilled in my life and in His kingdom when I embrace my gifts and personality. The more like me I am, the better I get at it.

WHERE AM I TO SERVE?

When I answered this question, the focus of my entire life shifted.

Because our chief purpose as Christians is to serve God, it makes sense that He should determine where we serve Him. It doesn't work when we say, "God, I'll be happy to serve you on Sunday in church. But the rest of the week is mine." When we identify our service to God as a separate component of our lives, then we misunderstand the Big Picture.

There is only one way to have a long-lasting, grounded approach to your life—and that is to know beyond a shadow of a doubt that God has called you to do what you are doing in all parts of your life. It's having a clear understanding of how your priorities align with God's priorities.

For many years, I believed my service to God was limited to church activities. I was an active member of my congregation, serving faithfully in children's and women's ministry. I was involved in the praise music team and believed that I would always be part of a music ministry.

When my husband wanted to move from Phoenix, Arizona, to Charlotte, North Carolina, I was not the picture of a respectful wife. In fact, I was just the opposite. I was a bitter, angry, and resentful woman. I was consumed with the injustice of the situation and what I saw as selfishness in my husband. I was convinced that moving was not in God's will for me. Even though my husband only wanted to move for two years, it made no difference. I continually asked myself, "How could he ask me to move across country and leave everything I love—my job, my church, my family?"

But somewhere deep inside I knew that my husband had never demanded his way in the past and, in fact, he wasn't demanding it then either. If I said no, we wouldn't move. But I also knew that if I said no, I would be squelching a dream he had had for many years, which was to live in a different city. That was not my dream. You see, I was born in Glendale, Arizona. My father taught at Glendale High School. I went to high school and college nearby, and at that time we lived within a half-mile of the Glendale city border. I wanted to stay right there close to my family and in surroundings I knew and loved.

My thoughts went something like this: "If I say no now, next time he wants to move it could be worse. And if I say no, he'll always resent me." And so I determined not to complain, said yes, and we moved. But in my heart, I was a mess. I'm ashamed to say that I believed my husband had stepped so far out of God's plan that I was destined to suffer for two years. While outwardly submissive, inwardly my heart was darkly rebellious. I decided to make the best of it, get through the next two years, and then return to my normal life. I believed when I returned to Arizona, I would go back to work and continue to serve God in my usual capacity.

But God had a decidedly different plan. God, in His ultimate mercy (and with His own brand of humor), introduced me to Proverbs 31 Ministries, a Christian organization based in Charlotte, with the calling "Touching Women's Hearts, Building Godly Homes." My heart needed more than touching at that time. It needed a good swat.

As I became involved in this ministry, God revealed that my view of my life and purpose was small compared to His. I had separated all the areas of my life and was destroying myself trying to keep everything balanced. Not only was I suffering, but I shortchanged everyone I loved, including God. It was as if my priorities were upside down.

As the truth of my identity in Christ became a reality in my life, I realized I was not the person God wanted me to be. The selfishness that was revealed in my move had been there all along. Even though my life looked good on the outside, the truth is that I was motivated by self-interest. Did my husband meet my needs? Did my children meet my needs? Did my church meet my needs? Did my job meet my needs? Me, me, me.

God pulled me out of the workplace and away from everything I loved to show me that it wasn't all about me. It was and is all about Jesus.

My life is to be a reflection of God's priorities. My primary area of ministry shifted from inside my church to inside my home. I know that I am called to be a godly wife and mother. After investing in my relationship with Christ, these are my top priorities. These are not areas of my life that deserve the leftovers of my energy and time.

Understand and pursue your calling.

God's priorities for me may be different than His priorities for you. But we both can discover God's unique call on our lives by staying plugged into God. Jesus modeled this for us in all He did. Even Jesus said, "I do nothing on my own but speak just what the Father has taught me" (John 8:28).

The only way to know what the Father wants to do in your life is to spend time alone with Him. God created you, equipped you, and He knows His calling on your life. Ask Him and He will reveal this part of His plan.

As you focus on who you are in Christ, what your purpose is, and how your entire life should be offered to God as an act of service, I believe God will reveal His will to you.

If you know God is calling you out of the workplace, pursue

this plan with enthusiasm and confidence. Don't let anything stand in your way to obeying God's call on your life.

As you begin this journey, remember to remain in close communication with the Lord. Renew your mind with the things of God so that you can discern God's will for you at each step.

"Commit to the Lord whatever you do, and your plans will succeed" (Proverbs 16:3).

CHAPTER 2

• • • • • • • •

THE REALITIES OF WORKING AT HOME

When I first started working at home, a former co-worker joked that my days would be filled with eating bonbons and watching soap operas. I wasn't sure what a bonbon was, but I did know the lure of soap operas. However, I found my days at home much too busy to live the pampered life he had imagined.

When I worked in the corporate world, I was guaranteed breaks and an hour lunch. Since my office was in an upscale retirement community with a full dining room, an employee benefit was low-cost lunches. Not only was the food fantastic, but I enjoyed the lunchroom conversations with friends, as well as the impromptu afterwork gatherings. There was excitement as we worked towards the completion of a project or celebrated the accomplishment of meeting a goal. I worked for wonderful people and their praise and encouragement fed my self-esteem.

Sounds great, doesn't it? It was. I really loved my job. My life looks very different now. My work breaks involve starting a load of laundry or cleaning the kitchen. Lunch consists of a reheated leftover or sandwich. Although my husband works at home, most days we each grab our lunch and each head back to work. My afterwork impromptu gatherings with friends are nonexistent, and for the most part I alone pat myself on the back when I've completed a task.

Would I ever go back to work outside the home? Not unless God sent me a personalized memo and told me so. I absolutely love being home.

What I didn't mention in my evaluation of being home includes snuggling on the couch with a child before he or she leaves for school; taking lunch to a child at school; volunteering to go on a field trip; having lunch with my mother; having dinner ready before the night's activities take over; and, just as important, *not* leaving the house before 7:00 each morning to get everyone to babysitters. These are just a few of the many benefits I enjoy every day being home.

Like most ventures, it's important to evaluate the pros and cons. Not that the cons should change your mind, but you'll proceed with eyes wide open. I've listed some of my favorite reasons for working at home and some of the challenges I've faced. You'll also find that chapter 16 deals with more emotional challenges of being home. May this information bring you encouragement and practical help if you experience similar issues.

The Positives of Working at Home
You'll have a more flexible work schedule.

It's a great feeling to get up early, grab a cup of coffee, and work for an hour before the kids get up. Even if it's just checking emails, my day is jump-started with that small amount of time. The next few hours are filled with getting the high schooler off, then the junior high son to jazz band practice, and the younger three leave an hour after that. Once they are gone, the kitchen is picked up, a load of laundry started, and I'm back to "work."

My husband, Tod, also works at home. Before he transitioned home, he left the house around 6:00 A.M., had an hour commute, worked all day, drove an hour home, and saw the kids for a few hours at night. That was when he was in town. Now, he still starts work around 6:00 A.M., but he tromps down the stairs to have cereal with someone, dashes over to school for lunch, and goes for a run or coaches baseball practice at 5:30 P.M.

While our days are full, the wonderful truth about working at home is we can schedule work around our lives, instead of our lives around our work. Because our work isn't tied to a clock, we can work at odd times of the day. That means sick kids aren't an inconvenience, school holidays aren't a concern, and a neighbor who needs a ride due to a dead battery isn't a major interruption.

You'll have more time for ministry and missions work.

Another benefit of working at home is you increase your availability to be used by God for ministry and missions work.

In the fall of 2005, my husband and I adopted two little sisters, Cathrine and Ruth, from Liberia, Africa. This wonderful happening came at the end of a wild year, which included the launch of two home-based businesses, my husband's transition home, and my first book contract.

As I consider that year, I'm convinced those happenings were connected with our more flexible schedules and our openness to be used by God in all areas of our lives.

Adoption is a long and laborious process. You hurry and fill out all the paperwork, then wait for months while it seems nothing is happening. Then, one day you receive a phone call announcing your daughters know they have been chosen for adoption and you can come get them in two weeks.

My husband and I stared mutely at each other and in 60 seconds decided that he would go. Those next two weeks were a whirlwind as we applied for Tod's visa, he got a physical and the necessary shots, and I tried to finish the girls' bedroom and guess at their clothing sizes. Two weeks later he flew to Africa and spent nine days there with the girls acquiring their American visas. My husband brought home two beautiful children, but left a piece of his heart in Africa. While there, God planted a vision in Tod to start a nonprofit organization to raise funds for the orphanage.

Tod will return to help build those precious children a school. This is a personal passion because Cathrine and Ruth had never even held a pencil before they came to us, and had never set foot in a school.

This missions work is easier because Tod is an entrepreneur who works from home. I know this might scare some of you who fear God might send you to Africa someday. If God does, trust me, you'll want to go. I tell you this story because when you offer your employment, your time, and your energy to God, prepare to be used. So many women and men who work from home find they are able to pursue more of God's kingdom work in their neighborhood, city, state, country, and world.

What an exciting by-product of working at home! But perhaps it's not a by-product after all. It's very possible that God is calling you to work at home primarily because He's got something else for you to do. Just consider it . . .

You'll experience an exciting opportunity for personal growth.

After a recent rain, I noticed the standing water in a garbage can had begun to smell. The stagnant water proved to be a breeding ground for all sorts of unpleasant beasties who enjoy that mucky environment. That can needed a blast of clean hose water to rinse away the foulness.

Anything stagnant for too long needs to be freshened up, and that includes personal growth. Working from home can open doors of opportunities to expand your knowledge, experience, and develop your strengths and character. Instead of moving from one status quo to another, consider this as a time of intentional personal growth.

You can grow in many different areas. When my friend Lynda started working from home, she read books about being a successful entrepreneur. She learned theories that changed her thinking about money and investments. She embraced teachings on leadership and leveraging your assets. Lynda's dedication to personal growth transformed her life and the lives of her daughters. Lynda continues to pursue growth and it shows in her success.

In an article entitled "Personal Growth," in his enewsletter *Leadership Wired,* John C. Maxwell, one of the nation's experts on leadership, says this: "I realized that to grow like I wanted, my personal development couldn't be hit-and-miss. I needed to initiate and activate. I made a decision to devote myself to personal growth. I literally made personal growth my personal mission."

In what area do you want to grow? Is it better time management? Organization? Do you want a broader knowledge of business practices? Marketing? Character development? Do you want deeper relationships? Leadership skills? Embrace this God-given chance and commit to growing in one or more areas.

Growth happens slowly and often unnoticed. It occurs in small increments and it can frustrate those of us who want it in big chunks and right now. When discouragement hits, remember the oak tree. Although the oak tree grows bit by bit and doesn't produce acorns for at least 20 years, it is universally known as a strong and faithful tree. It's a tree that can be counted on to survive the storms, support tree houses, and provide shade for generations. While our lifespan is substantially shorter than the oak's, we can strive to mirror its solid growth and long-standing faithfulness.

The Challenges of Working at Home
It's really hard work.

When I first worked at home, my youngest son was only four. Little Robbie definitely preferred my company to playing alone. He loves physical touch and wanted to be held often. Consequently, when we were together, my concentration was on him. Because of his personality and needs, on most days, it would have been easier to work outside my home than to get something done at home.

Having children to care for is only one reason working at home is challenging. It's also difficult
- to know when to stop;
- to separate work and home;
- to put in all the extra hours you need to start a business;
- to work when you'd rather watch the Food Network;

- to learn aspects of the business world that were formerly unknown to you;
- to lovingly explain to children, parents, friends, and family that you need to work, even though you are home;
- to say no to volunteering at the school carnival because you have a deadline to meet;
- to fight the guilt when you say no because you're sure everyone is wondering why you don't have the time since you work at home.

When I start feeling overwhelmed by the demands, I force myself to take a break. I refocus on God and His promise to never leave me. I remember that God offers to give me wisdom, protection, strength, and encouragement if I only ask. Then I remember I haven't asked God lately for those things, and go to Him in prayer.

Yes, working at home is difficult, at times overwhelming, but we have a God who is able to help. The author of Hebrews encourages us with these words when we are weak:

For we do not have a high priest who is unable to sympathize with our weaknesses, but we have one who has been tempted in every way, just as we are—yet was without sin. Let us then approach the throne of grace with confidence, so that we may receive mercy and find grace to help us in our time of need (Hebrews 4:15–17).

There is a danger of workaholism.

Psychotherapist Bryan E. Robinson, author of *Chained to the Desk: A Guidebook for Workaholics, Their Partners and Children, and the Clinicians Who Treat Them,* calls workaholism the "best-dressed addiction in the United States." It's depicted by the worker who feels a compulsion to work and who finds it hard, if not impossible, to engage in her personal life. Let the warning bell sound now, because if you have trouble with workaholism working outside your home, it will increase at home.

John Maxwell, in an article entitled "Work Addiction" in his enewsletter *Leadership Wired,* warns about this problem: "The work addict has lost the fundamental ability to disconnect and disengage from the demands of the office. Aside from personal health concerns, workaholism negatively affects job performance by depriving work addicts of rest and rendering them powerless to meet new challenges with the necessary energy reserves to solve complex problems."

The unfortunate aspect of workaholism is that many see it as something to be desired rather than avoided. In the workplace, the workaholic may rise to the top of his or her profession and be envied or admired by others. However, this obsessive need to work often masks deeper emotional issues. While the workaholic may succeed in the short-run, there inevitably will be some type of breakdown—whether relational, physical, spiritual, or emotional.

Robinson, whose private practice is in Asheville, North Carolina, conducted research at the University of North Carolina at Charlotte and found the divorce rate among workaholics is 40 percent higher than the rest of the population. Workaholics also suffer physical ailments, such as headaches, exhaustion, and muscle tension.

Work is God-ordained. The Scriptures advise us, "Whatever you do, work at it with all your heart, as working for the Lord" (Colossians 3:23).

But work was never designed to fulfill all of our needs. To overcome the obsession with work, spend some time evaluating your priorities in life: your personal relationship with Jesus, your family relationships, your health, your home, and so on. Seek to establish a balance by investing an equal measure of your time and energy into your top priorities.

Start by setting some boundaries, such as turning off your computer and cell phone at a certain time each day, not working one day a week, and scheduling exercise or time with loved ones. Facing the issue honestly, seeking accountability from others, and taking small steps to balance your life can address workaholism. However, for those who are unable to handle their obsession, professional Christian counseling should be considered.

You will battle fear.

It was a warm autumn night as I watched my sons practice football. Three other mothers and I lounged in our chairs, alternately glancing at the practice to make sure we saw the tackles and passes and discussing the frustration of preparing dinner on busy weeknights.

As we talked I discovered that all three of them worked full-time outside their homes. These devoted moms really wanted to prepare nutritious meals, but it was all they could do to race home from work, grab a quick snack, and then race to practice. After practice they returned home exhausted and reached for another quick-fix item for dinner.

When the conversation turned to me, I shared that because I work at home I was able to make an early dinner. After that, each woman expressed her desire to be home during the day, and in almost the same breath declared why she couldn't do it. My heart broke with compassion because I saw the sense of helplessness in their words and facial expressions. It was as if they were resigned to a full-time job, and that was that.

My three football-practice friends are like hundreds of thousands of women across the country who wish they could stay home but don't think it's possible. All they see is one obstacle after another. They see a mountain of debt, the problem of health insurance, a child's empty college fund, an unsupportive spouse, or a workplace that "needs" them.

What these women don't see is a God who can handle all those obstacles. Instead of trusting God to provide, they work harder and longer to make ends meet. But the ends just get farther apart.

Psalm 20:7 says, "Some trust in chariots and some in horses, but we trust in the name of the LORD our God." Although that was written thousands of years ago, I wonder if we sometimes underestimate God's capabilities and trust in our own "horses" and "chariots." We may have a head knowledge about trusting God, but in reality we trust in a company, or our physical strength, or our intelligence.

I've found that sometimes God waits for us to make the first

work @ home

move in faith, believing that He will take care of us. Exodus 14 tells of the Israelites' escape from the Egyptian army. As the terrified Israelites get to the edge of the sea, with more than 600 chariots on their heels, they cry out to God and complain to Moses. They are so afraid of the future that they express a desire to be back in slavery in Egypt. Here's what the Scriptures say:

As Pharaoh approached, the Israelites looked up, and there were the Egyptians, marching after them. They were terrified and cried out to the LORD. They said to Moses, "Was it because there were no graves in Egypt that you brought us to the desert to die? What have you done to us by bringing us out of Egypt? Didn't we say to you in Egypt, 'Leave us alone; let us serve the Egyptians'? It would have been better for us to serve the Egyptians than to die in the desert!" —Exodus 14:10–12

Moses is a good leader, and instead of answering back sarcastically, "No, there weren't anymore graves in Egypt! Start digging!" as I might have done, he reminds the people of God's faithfulness:

Moses answered the people, "Do not be afraid. Stand firm and you will see the deliverance the LORD will bring you today. The Egyptians you see today you will never see again. The LORD will fight for you; you need only to be still" (Exodus 10:13–14).

Moses is patient and encouraging, but God's answer in the next verse is a bit different in tone: "Then the LORD said to Moses, 'Why are you crying out to me? Tell the Israelites to move on.'"

To sum up the situation, the Israelites are following God's leading to a promised land, they've seen Him perform miracles to set them free, and they stand there complaining, frozen in fear, and resigned to die. All the while God is waiting for them to *just move!* You see, sometimes we just have to do something in spite of the fear.

Is God asking you to trust Him today? Is He saying to you, "I've heard your cries. I know you want to be home. It's now time for you to *move on* and make it happen"?

Satan would like fear to be our constant companion. Satan would like us to believe that we aren't smart enough, capable enough, skilled enough, resourceful enough, hardworking enough. But God says, "I am enough for you!"

Whatever fear you battle regarding working at home, God is enough. I once heard someone say, "If your problem is too big, then your God is too small." There is no problem or challenge you face today or will face in the future that will surprise God. He is always prepared with a way around, over, or through your problem. I pray with all my heart that you discover God in a whole new and delightful way as you begin to work from home. May His faithfulness be a blanket of comfort when fear tries to sneak into your heart and dissuade you from your purpose.

CHAPTER 3

· · · · · · · ·

INVOLVING THE FAMILY

When I worked outside my home full-time, I focused fully on my job. My husband was occupied at work and my kids were safe and well cared for at school or day care. While the phone might ring with a concern from one or another, I was basically on my own until 5:00 in the evening. My career development depended on my ability to make it happen. I signed up for conferences, took out-of-town assignments, and worked late without much effort.

My public relations career was just that—mine. While the support of my family was important, it wasn't required for my day-to-day performance at work. Working from home, however, is a book with a different cover. The support of my family isn't an option, it's an absolute necessity.

Before making the move home, spend some time working through the details with your spouse and children. There are often unrealistic expectations from all parties involved. There's a stereotype of a woman working at home that looks something like this:

No alarm is needed for this work-at-home woman. She

rises when she's fulfilled her need for sleep. Everyone gets a homecooked breakfast, complete with biscuits and gravy. The kids get a creative sack lunch every day with sandwiches cut in the shapes of animals. Once everyone has left for the day, she saunters to her desk, still in her pajamas and coffee mug in hand. She holds a happy baby on her knee and does an hour of work. After which she does the laundry, cleans the bathroom (baby is still happy), takes a lunch break with friends, then does more work before the older kids get home. Everyone gets one-on-one homework help, dinner is on the table at 5:30, and the night winds down after that.

This sounds like a setting for a 1950s sitcom, not the real life of a woman working at home. Working at home can include those components, but life doesn't always flow that smoothly. Real life is more like this:

The alarm goes off at 5:30 A.M. as our work-at-home heroine arises before her family. She tries to get some work done before anyone wakes up, but is surprised by a toddler who wants to be held. She holds the curious two-year-old on her lap while editing a report, but his little hands grope for the keyboard. By pressing a rare combination of keys only advanced programmers know, he somehow disables the CD-ROM and sound from the computer. By now the other kids are up and our working woman hurries to get breakfast ready and lunches packed. She looks up to see the six-year-old happily coloring on some paper she found. A familiar logo catches her eye and she realizes her little artist is decorating a contract for an important job. The day proceeds in much the same fashion. Our hardworking woman struggles to balance the needs of her child at home, the phone calls, her employer's request for overdue work, her husband's surprise plans for the evening, and her need for peace.

Even the most supportive family members will have trouble understanding why you can't get everything done now that you are home. A little preparatory groundwork can save you conflict down the road. This groundwork will include prayer and serious discussions about the ramifications of making this transition. The most important place to start the discussion is with your husband.

Receive your husband's blessing.

After confirming God's call on your life to work at home, if you are married, the next step is to receive your husband's blessing and support. If your husband has been asking you to work from home for years, then you're in great shape. You can proceed with your plans joyfully and hand in hand with your husband. This agreement will ease all your discussions about potentially explosive issues like finances.

Adapt when he doesn't agree.

However, if your husband is uncertain about whether this is a good idea or if he's set against it, you'll need to approach the subject very differently. Before saying anything more, spend dedicated time in prayer. Pray like the psalmist: "Search me, O God, and know my heart; test me and know my anxious thoughts. See if there is any offensive way in me, and lead me in the way everlasting" (Psalm 139:23–24).

When I'm excited about a new idea and my husband isn't, I can easily start down a path of thoughts that aren't pleasing to the Lord. Once a negative thought has taken root, it affects my words and behavior. Before you start a shouting match with your husband, listing all the reasons why you should work at home and why he's a fool if he doesn't agree, make sure your heart is in the right place. Confess any thoughts of anger, hatred, resentment, selfishness, and unforgivingness.

I'm confident the Lord cares more about our hearts than our actions. We can do and say all the right things; but if we are seething inside, God isn't very happy with us. So, if you have a resistant husband, drop the matter until your heart is in the right place.

We live in the middle of a spiritual battleground. Satan would like very much to put a wedge between you and your husband. Take the first move to disarm the enemy by putting your thought life under the dominion of Christ. The apostle Paul knew the importance of thoughts and the power of Jesus. In 2 Corinthians 10:3–5 (NASB) he advises:

For though we walk in the flesh, we do not war according to the flesh, for the weapons of our warfare are not of the flesh, but divinely powerful for the destruction of fortresses. We are destroying speculations and every lofty thing raised up against the knowledge of God, and we are taking every thought captive to the obedience of Christ.

Be respectful.

Once you've got your emotions under control and your heart in submission to Christ, you can again approach the topic of working at home with your husband. Arrange to meet when you are free from distractions and interruptions and when you both have a block of time to talk. Make sure there are no other pressing concerns which will weigh heavily on your husband's mind.

As you begin your conversation, make sure your heart and words are bathed in respect for your husband. Whether he acknowledges it or not, your husband longs for your respect—it's in his God-given makeup. Whether you think he deserves it or not—you wives are asked to respect your husbands. Ephesians 5:33 states, "However, each one of you also must love his wife as he loves himself, and the wife must respect her husband."

Without your respect, your husband is sure to react negatively. Author Emerson E. Eggerichs calls this "the crazy cycle." In an article entitled, "Research Shows the Reality of the Crazy Cycle," Eggerichs writes, "Without love a wife reacts without respect, and without respect a husband reacts without love. . . . Things get crazy because this feeds itself. Her disrespect feeds his lack of love. His unloving reactions feed her disrespect. Round and round it goes."

By being aware this might happen, you can stop the cycle by choosing respectful words, facial expressions, and tone of voice in your conversation. You might not agree with your husband, but you can respect his God-given position as leader of your family.

Choose the right approach.

Much conflict between men and women comes down to differing methods of exchanging ideas. In Sharon Jayne's book,

Becoming the Woman of His Dreams, she describes our differences in communication styles:

When it comes to understanding how a man's mind works in the words department, reading the newspaper is an effective exercise. A trained newspaper reporter will give the article a catchy title, and then he or she will list the important facts of the article in the first few sentences. If you are intrigued, you'll read more. If not, you've got the gist of the situation in the first paragraph and that may be enough.

Bingo. That's how the male mind wants to receive information. First get his attention. Give him a title. (*I need to talk to you about our son wrecking the car last night.*) Give him the main points. (*He was driving your car, exceeding the speed limit by 20 miles per hour, and hit a fence.*) Then, move along to the other paragraphs of interest such as the ramifications and emotions. (*I am furious and think we should take the keys away from him for a month, make him pay for the damages, and insist he take the driver's safety class for the next four Saturdays.*)

We can take Sharon's example and apply it when discussing working at home. Sharon offers the following suggestions for approaching your husband on this topic:

Give the main idea first. (*I would like to talk to you about working from home.*) Elaborate where needed. (*I've done my research and found that in actuality, I am only bringing home $50 a week. All the other money from my paycheck is going toward day care, eating out, parking, transportation, and clothes.*) Finally, address the emotional ramifications at the end. (*I feel that I could be a better wife and mother if I had more energy to focus on our family's needs. As it is now, I have so little to give emotionally at the end of the day.*)

To round out the discussion, be prepared by completing the Cost of Working Outside the Home analysis provided at the end of chapter 4. This will show your husband you've done your research.

The other side of the conversation will include how you will make money at home. It would be good to have examples of possible telecommuting jobs or information about home-based businesses.

Avoid saying what you might regret.

Because our goal is to have our husbands in willing agreement, it's best to avoid tactics involving guilt or shame. Depending on the makeup of your husband, these manipulative techniques may or may not work. Even if you know your tears can sway your husband, don't go there. You may get a preliminary agreement, but it won't have lasting value. You don't want to always resort to drama to get your way.

Even though you may be very emotional over this topic, especially if you have children, try to keep your emotions in check. Women tend to move from logic to emotions very easily, while men can stay logical. To keep the playing ground level, so to speak, pause before you say something you might regret.

Also, don't make promises you can't keep. Don't promise to have his shirts always ironed, the dinner ready at a specific time, or the kids spit-shined when he walks in the door at the end of the day. As you read the rest of this book, you'll get a better picture of the realities of working at home. Be cautious about your commitments. Simply promise to do your very best, to be faithful to your commitments, and to love and honor your husband and children.

Suggest a trial period.

If your husband is still hesitant about the transition, offer to try it for six months to a year, with the understanding that you'll return to work outside the home if not successful. If he agrees, you've got yourself a challenge. Set a realistic time frame in which to make it work, depending on how you intend to make money. If you are starting a from-scratch, home-based business, expect your trial time to take at least a year. If telecommuting or starting a direct-sales business, you can try it for a short period of time, as you should create income more quickly.

Suggest a compromise.

An alternate idea might be to reduce your employment hours to part-time and start working at home part-time. You can do this for little financial investment with a direct-sales business. Of course, you won't spend any money at all to get set up if you work out a part-time telecommuting alternative with your current employer.

As your work-at-home arrangement is successful, I believe your husband will see your dedication to your work and family and will be open to a full-time transition.

Accept his decision if he says no.

If your husband just isn't ready for you to work at home, then accept his decision with grace. There could be many reasons for his answer, and perhaps he can't even communicate them. If you do get a no, then guard your heart against resentment and unforgivingness. Do not allow this decision to destroy your relationship.

Two reasons for a no answer come to mind. The first is a concern over money. This may be a legitimate reason for delaying a transition. Along with your husband, take a good look at your budget. If you find yourself getting deeper in debt, then work at reducing the debt and expenses so your husband is more comfortable with your financial situation. If your schedule allows, you might consider working at home while working your current job. That way, you can pay down your credit cards or increase your savings until the time comes when you can fully work at home.

The second reason for no is that your husband may not believe you have the skills to work at home or run a business. If your husband can verbalize his reasons, then pray about how you can respond to his concerns to increase his confidence.

Proverbs 31 is a biblical picture of a wife who inspires trust in her husband. Verses 11 and 12 say, "Her husband has full confidence in her and lacks nothing of value. She brings him good, not harm, all the days of her life." The chapter goes on to list many of the ways this entrepreneurial woman inspires confidence and brings her husband good:

- She has a noble character.
- She provides food for her family.
- She plans with an eye to the future.
- She's hardworking.
- She speaks with wisdom.
- She watches over the affairs of all her household.
- She cares for her children.
- She loves and honors the Lord.

While we may not do everything that ideal Proverbs 31 woman did, we can aspire to some of the principles represented in the chapter. If you need help in this area, I'd love to recommend Proverbs 31 Ministries. Proverbs 31 is a national ministry with the goal to support women in finding balance in their busy lives and following the principles outlined in this chapter. To learn more, visit their Web site at www.proverbs31.org.

Communicate the change to your children.

I don't think you'll need to do any convincing with your children. You'll spend more time answering their excited questions than talking them into the idea. I do believe you'll need to communicate clearly what to expect; otherwise, you'll have very disappointed offspring. Above all, just as with your husband, don't make promises you don't know you can keep. I learned this years ago.

One day, just before the start of school, my middle son sat cross-legged on the floor, playing at the foot of my desk while I worked on the computer. He wasn't a typical six-year-old, so I shouldn't have been surprised at his comment. "Mom," he started simply. "When you were little, did Grandma ever tell you she'd get you a pony and then didn't?"

"No, she didn't," I answered, fully engaged and wondering where this line of thought would go.

"Well, you told us you'd take us to Toys 'R' Us this summer and you didn't. That's a true lie," Dylan solidly proclaimed.

I was shocked that he remembered a promise from three months back, but more stunned by his reasoning. He was right. Every time we drove past the toy store, they'd ask and I'd put them off. It wasn't that we didn't have the time, but taking three little boys into a toy store was pure torture. Either I should have taken them or I shouldn't have promised we would do it.

You'll be tempted to paint a wonderful picture where you'll take the kids to the park in the afternoons or have lunch with them at school once a week. That may happen, and you can set it as a goal, just don't promise you'll do it. There are always circumstances beyond our control, but most kids don't understand that. All many see is a parent who didn't keep her word.

Dealing with the reality of Mom working at home is an ongoing process at our house. Just when I thought my three boys understood my responsibilities and need for quiet at times, we adopted two little girls from Africa. Their communication skills are similar to preschoolers, so they just don't understand that even though I'm in the room, they can't talk to me all the time. As my children enter different phases of their lives, I'm challenged to adapt to their needs. It sure keeps me on my toes.

Build family unity.

Everyone has a need to belong and to feel part of something bigger than themselves. Your transition home can be the catalyst for creating family unity. Communicate your long-term dreams with your husband and children and let them know how much you need their support. When you experience a success, share it with them. Don't forget to thank them for their help. If your daughter played quietly while you finished a major project, take time to express your gratitude. Also, consider if there are small ways kids can help. Even if it's punching holes or stapling, let your children contribute to your work.

This is an exciting time in the life of your family. You can grow individually and together as you set goals, work to reach them, and then celebrate the accomplishments. If you've never had family devotions or meetings, this might be a time to start. Take time to discuss your schedules for the week, read Scripture, share an inspiring thought, and pray. God may be opening up a whole new chapter for your family through your obedience of working at home.

CHAPTER 4

· · · · · · · ·

THE REAL COST OF WORK

Susan was a teacher and loved her job. But the situation at home was changing. She and her new husband had their first child. Within the next three years, her three adolescent stepdaughters moved in.

While this was reason for celebration, it also was a source of significant stress. A new marriage; caring for a toddler, one preteen, and two teenage girls; and a time-consuming job were wearing on Susan. After a few years of juggling everyone's needs, she was near exhaustion and knew something had to give.

When a new school year started, Susan was asked to take on some difficult assignments without adequate help. The accumulated stress of the past years overtook her. Every day she cried as she began her ten-mile commute to work. She dreaded leaving her family and she dreaded going to work. Knowing she had waited too long, she took the steps necessary to resign.

It was about that time Susan and her husband, Steve, joined an evening small group studying how to successfully transition out of the workplace. As part of the study, they created an assessment of the cost of working outside the home. The results astounded them both. After identifying an assortment of expenses, they discovered it actually *cost* Susan $200 a year to work!

Susan didn't have unusually high work-related expenses. She did pay for child care. As a teacher of young children, perhaps her clothes needed replacing more often due to markers, paint, and chocolate pudding hugs. And, as most teachers know, the money for many classroom supplies came out of Susan's pocket.

This cost-to-work assessment was a confirmation of Susan's decision to quit. With a closer eye on the budget, Susan and Steve managed well on one income. Although there have been some challenges and watching of pennies, four years later Susan is still home and loving it.

While Susan and Steve's experience might be the exception, it does reveal that the costs associated with working outside the home are more numerous than you might think. Some are obvious, but many are hidden and difficult to identify.

The Two-Income Myth

If you believe today's culture, families need two incomes to survive. On the surface, this seems to be true. Housing and transportation expenses are increasing, quality child care is expensive, and then there is credit card debt. It would seem that families "need" two incomes to make ends meet, plus have extra to raise their standard of living.

In their book *The Two-Income Trap,* authors Elizabeth Warren and Amelia Warren Tyagi state that two-income families today earn 75 percent more in inflation-adjusted dollars than their one-income counterparts of a generation ago, but have less discretionary income.

In addition, according to the Administrative Office of the US Courts, more than 2 million people filed for bankruptcy in fiscal year 2005, which is a 30 percent jump over 2004 numbers. Bankruptcies have increased 98 percent in federal courts since 1994. And 9 million people are in credit counseling.

The Bureau of Labor Statistics reported in 2004 that 61 percent of families with children have two adults working. So why are so many of them struggling to make ends meet?

The answers are simple, yet difficult to live by. In general, Americans spend too much on necessities (such as housing, food, and clothing), are in too much debt, and suffer from a severe lack of personal accountability.

It's easy to blame our financial situations on increasing costs of living or on societal pressures to own more goods. I could blame the credit card companies that send me at least two preapproved applications a day. Or it could be the fault of the ads on television, which use subtle and not-so-subtle persuasion to convince me I need a new outfit, car, or house in a better neighborhood.

But the truth is there are married couples living well on one middle-class income, and there are single parents who manage to work from home. It takes determination and self-control—two personal characteristics that need intentional focus and help from the Holy Spirit to flourish in our lives.

For Christians, we have the benefit of the Holy Spirit who lives in us and can work in us to bring wisdom and self-control. Galatians 5:22 tells us we know when we are living according to God's design because our lives reflect what is called the fruit of the Spirit—love, joy, peace, patience, kindness, goodness, faithfulness, gentleness, and self-control. Christian character traits, including self-control, are produced by the Holy Spirit, not through the desperate attempts of trying to live by our own strength.

This is one reason it's hard to make sacrificial decisions—we try to do it on our own strength, and fail. And it's also why there are many people still working in the traditional workplace when God is calling them home. It takes sacrifice. But it can be done.

Assessing Your Cost to Work

Whether you are married or single, the first place to start in making the transition home is uncovering the real cost of work. When you take a detailed look at work-related expenses, you'll discover if you can afford to live on one income, or you'll learn what you need to make from home to replace your net income.

Before you start, gather pertinent information like pay stubs and receipts of expenses if you have them. Sometimes your check register can work just as well if you record debits and ATM transactions as well as checks.

There are some great calculators online that will walk you through this process, but an old-fashioned pencil and paper work great too. Crown Financial Ministries' Web site (www.crown.org) offers an easy to understand cost-to-work calculator. Check under Tools on their home page.

Step 1: Determine your net spendable income.

The first step involves identifying your net spendable income. I think it's easier to work on a monthly basis, so start by finding your gross monthly income. Your gross income is how much you make before taxes or any other withdrawals, such as insurance or retirement investments.

Then you'll need to subtract some non-negotiables. There are four main expenses: federal tax, state tax, Social Security tax, and our tithe back to God. The first three should be found on your paycheck stub.

A big expense for all Americans is income tax. Unfortunately, the federal tax system is set up so that in a two-income family, both incomes are added together to determine the tax bracket. For example, if one earner makes $30,000, which is in the 15 percent federal tax bracket, and the second earner makes $14,000, which is in the 10 percent tax brackets, both incomes are taxed at their combined bracket, which would be 15 percent.

When considering possible savings in a two-earner family, consider if the first income would drop into a lower tax bracket without the second income tacked on.

State income tax varies by state. You'll need to do some research to determine your state's policy.

Social Security tax is based on a simple idea. While you work, you pay taxes into the Social Security system; and when you retire or become disabled, you, your spouse, and your dependent children receive monthly benefits based on your reported earnings. Also, your survivors can collect benefits if you die. Normally, the employer pays part and you pay part. In 2004, the tax rate for an employee was 7.65 percent.

Another substantial expense is the tithe on the second income. For families who give 10 percent of their income, this can be an area where you will "save" money. Of course, every Christian needs to ask the Lord what He would have them do in this area. We should give with a cheerful heart, and not look for opportunities to "save" in the area of giving. However, if you feel called to give 10 percent of your income and your income drops, this would be a financial expense that will change.

For an income of $20,400, or $1,700 a month, these four expenses can add up to just over $600, or 35 percent. If the first wage earner is in a significantly higher tax bracket than the second, the total can be even higher.

When you have subtracted taxes and tithe, you will come up with your net spendable monthly income. This is what you have left to spend on the expenses of life.

Step 2: Identify your work-related expenses.

As you work your way towards your net income, the next step is to identify your work-related expenses. These are expenses you would not have if you were at home, such as child care and commuting.

Child care. This is a huge expense for parents. Costs can range greatly from state to state, and depend on the age and number of your children. Monthly rates range from $400 to $2,000 a month per child. Even if you pay a family member a small amount, include that as an expense.

If you were planning to put your child in preschool, then add only the cost of afterschool care.

Transportation. With rising gas prices, the commute to work is becoming a significant expense in a family's monthly budget.

With a 20-mile round trip commute in a midsized car, you can expect to pay between $75 and $150 a month if you work full-time. That allows some money for insurance, plus general wear and tear on your vehicle and tires. Add more if you use your car for other business trips during the day and aren't reimbursed. Don't forget to add in parking costs if applicable.

Depending on the miles driven to work, some automobile insurance rates rise when a vehicle is used in a commute. Since you would purchase automobile insurance whether or not you work, only include the extra expense necessary to use your car for commuting purposes. This information can be found by calling your insurance agent.

Meals and snacks during work. When I worked full-time, I would often treat myself to lunch at a restaurant or spend extra money on snacks and drinks. The busyness of doing all the nightly chores and then getting kids ready for day care the next morning eliminated any extra time or energy I had to consistently make myself a sack lunch.

You will probably have to estimate these expenses, as they tend to slip through the cracks. Count up how many coffees you grab as you drive to work, snacks from a vending machine, and lunch or afterwork outings with co-workers.

Clothing. My work-at-home wardrobe consists of shorts and T-shirts in the summer and comfortable pants and warm shirts in the winter. When I worked full-time, I wore a completely different set of clothes. I needed to maintain a professional appearance and purchased suits, skirts, dresses, and nicer shoes than the slippers I wear at home. Some jobs require a uniform.

Try to estimate how much you spend annually on clothing, uniforms, shoes, hosiery, and jewelry that you wouldn't normally buy for everyday at-home wear. Then divide that number by 12 to get your monthly clothing expense.

Dry cleaning. Not only do work clothes cost more to buy, but they cost more to maintain. How much do you spend every month at the dry cleaners? If there is money spent on laundering and ironing men's work shirts, consider what you would save if you did that at home.

Personal grooming/services. This applies more to women than men, but we all need to look our best when we are in the workforce. On many jobs, first impressions are important. Consider the cost of personal supplies and services such as professional manicures, acrylic nails, pedicures, makeup, hair care, and perfume or cologne.

Is your job so stressful that you need a massage once a month? Include that too.

It is possible that you will need two massages once you are home! But let's cross that bridge when we get to it.

Business gifts. Ah, the office gift for the boss! Or the Christmas gift exchange, baby shower, wedding shower, and birthdays. The list goes on. When I worked, it seemed every month there was something else to celebrate. This helps to cement the camaraderie in the workplace, but it can get expensive.

Co-workers and bosses can put subtle pressure on you to join these gift-giving experiences, and often you might believe you'll be blackballed if you don't participate. There's freedom in being able to give gifts to your friends without pressure.

Step 3: Estimate expenses that could be avoided by being home.

Some expenses are hard to nail down as directly related to work. You might not be able to list these when you create your cost assessment. But if you can, then by all means include them in your list.

Home maintenance. When you are working outside the home, your time may be more valuable than money. You may engage the help of a housecleaner, gardener, or painter. Consider what tasks you might be able to assume if you had more time at home.

Meals out. It's a fact of life that after a busy workday, few people want to go home and prepare, cook, and clean up after a meal. I hardly want to do it and I'm home! It's much easier to order a pizza or swing by a fast-food restaurant. I was shocked to learn that McDonald's is the source of 10 percent of family meals. I've bought my share of chicken nuggets, but that's amazing.

You can probably identify times when you might have eaten at home if you had more time or energy. Then, estimate how much you might spend in a month.

Another work-related expense is having your kids buy their breakfast and/or lunches at school or day care. It's often easier to buy a prepackaged lunch from the grocery store rather than making it ourselves. Count up how many prepackaged lunches you've bought in the last month.

Guilt gifts to children. We may not readily admit it, but we can feel guilty when we've been away from our kids all week. "They deserve a treat," we think.

These guilt gifts might take the form of actual gifts, such as a "little something" picked up on a business trip or extra-large or multiple gifts at birthdays or Christmas. More money can be spent on special outings that you otherwise might not take, just so you can spend time together without interruptions.

Increased health-care costs. When my second son was under two, he was in full-time day care. During those first years we made numerous trips to the doctor's office for colds and ear infections. In fact, it was so bad that two times we came close to putting tubes in his ears. In contrast, my third son, who didn't go to day care, was relatively sickness free. While this isn't always the case, there is an increased risk of exposure to sickness when children are placed in group situations early in life.

Although the signs clearly say, "Please keep sick kids home," working parents will send their precious little runny-nosed baby to day care and school. That's just the truth. Even if *most* times you stay home with a sick child, there's occasionally a meeting you just can't miss. And so your child may stay sick longer, and other children are infected with a nasty bug.

Sometimes the stresses of balancing home and career are too much for adults and their immune system is weakened, resulting in increased health problems. This category is difficult to assign a dollar amount, but it's worth considering as you count the costs of working outside the home.

Miscellaneous. You might have expenses this chapter hasn't mentioned. Perhaps there are professional dues, extra education, or workshops you need to attend. Consider if you have to purchase books, special electronic equipment, or maintain your own cell phone or beeper. There are all kinds of little expenses that pop up throughout the year.

If some of these expenses occur only once a year, add them together and divide by 12 to get your monthly expense.

The final step: add, subtract, and determine what you really bring home.

When you've got a list of all your monthly work-related expenses, add them up and subtract that number from your net spendable income. This is what you really bring home from your job.

When you look at that number, you have to decide how you are going to make it up once you are home. You might discover that you can save that amount by shopping smarter or reducing expenses by moving to a smaller house or apartment. You may be able to eliminate some debt before you quit and realize that you don't need to make it up at all.

I'll be discussing various work-at-home options in later chapters.

Cost-to-Work Assessment

While some expenses are obvious, others are hidden. At the end of the month we might wonder, "Where did all the money go?" By taking the time to do a cost-to-work assessment, you have begun to paint a realistic picture of your current financial situation.

In the next chapter, we'll take a look at how to create a budget that will allow you to fulfill your dream of being home.

Cost of Working Outside the Home
Sample Work Sheet

<u>Monthly Gross Income</u>	$3,750
(based on annual salary of $45,000)	
(based on married filing jointly)	
Tithe	375
Federal Taxes (15%)	563
State Taxes (vary; for sample 3.74%)	140
Social Security Taxes (7.65%)	286
<u>Net Monthly Income</u>	$2,386
Cost-of-Work Expenses	
Child care	750
Transportation	110
Meals/Coffee/Snacks ($5.00 a day average)	100
Takeout/Meals out at home	200
Clothes	150
Hair/Nails	75
Miscellaneous expenses	150
Parking at work	
Dry cleaning	
Gifts at work	
Kid's hot lunches rather than sack	
Total Expenses	$1,535
Spendable income	$851

Cost of Working Outside the Home
Personal Work Sheet

Monthly Gross Income _____

Tithe _____
Federal Taxes _____
State Taxes _____
Social Security Taxes _____

Net Monthly Income _____
    Cost-of-Work Expenses
    Child care _____
    Transportation _____
    Meals/Coffee/Snacks _____
    Takeout/Meals out at home _____
    Clothes _____
    Hair/Nails _____

Miscellaneous expenses _____
    Parking at work
    Dry cleaning
    Gifts at work
    Kid's hot lunches rather than sack

Total Expenses _____

Monthly Gross Income _____
Subtract Total Expenses - _____
Spendable income = _____

CHAPTER 5
· · · · · · · ·

PREPARING A FAMILY BUDGET

God cares how we manage our money. In fact, Jesus taught more on money than He did on heaven or hell. There are more than 2,000 biblical references to money, wealth, possessions, and money principles. In fact, next to salvation, stewardship is the second greatest theme of the Bible. The Bible is full of information on financial management, because it matters to God.

Jesus said, "For where your treasure is, there your heart will be also" (Matthew 6:21). A review of our checkbooks and calendars will quickly reveal where our treasures reside. Are our money and time spent on pleasure or overindulgence, or are they spent on the things of God?

As we spend some time reviewing budgeting, it's important to consider the spiritual ramifications of our decisions. Most people who transition out of the workplace will experience a reduced income for a period of time. When that happens, we often need to revise our budgets. Your response to the questions of where to save and what to cut from your budget will reveal where your heart is. It's OK if you discover your heart is far from God's will for your finances. Don't give up. Just don't stay there!

If the Holy Spirit reveals some weaknesses or sin as you read this chapter, I encourage you to confess those things to God. First John 1:9 tells us, "If we confess our sins, he is faithful and just and will forgive us our sins and purify us from all unrighteousness." I'm confident that with God's power you can be set free from any sinful habits concerning your money. When that happens, you'll have quite a testimony.

In chapter 4, you spent some time analyzing the real cost for you to work outside your home. In doing so, you took the first step toward a realistic look at what income you'll need to make once you are home.

In the example I prepared, the employee's gross income was $3,750 a month. After subtracting the tithe, taxes, and costs associated with working outside the home, she actually brought home $851 spendable dollars towards living expenses each month.

At the family's current level of debt and expenses, this individual will need to make $851 working from home just to survive. That's assuming the family was paying their bills and wasn't getting into deeper debt each month using credit cards. If that's the case, then the individual will need to make drastic changes to reverse the debt cycle.

Other chapters in this book will address ways to make that money or save money, but before we move into those arenas, we need to address wise financial stewardship and how to manage money. The foundation for wisdom in this area of our life is godly, biblical planning of a budget. Good planning always starts with an understanding of why. Why do you even need a budget?

Why Have a Budget?

The ultimate goal of a budget is to help us practice biblical stewardship. Biblical financial stewardship means wisely caring for the resources God entrusts to us. The truth is, God has given us whatever amount of money we have. It may look like we earned it by working hard, but the source of our income is the Lord.

Biblical stewardship encompasses so much more than making sure our checkbooks balance at the end of the month. Plenty of folks are wise financial managers without ever putting their expenses on paper. They know stewardship starts in the heart and that reveals itself through everyday actions. They've learned to care for the money God entrusted to them by living in moderation, planning for the future, and avoiding debt.

For those who haven't been good stewards of money, a budget is the primary tool for getting on the right track. It's the first step to taking control over their finances, instead of being a servant to them. Before we dive into the mechanics of a budget, let's start with God's heart towards money.

It's God's money.

There are very important reasons for Christians to budget their money. As I just mentioned, it's not really our money. It's God's money and we are stewards of it. For us to grasp the importance of money management, we need to get this truth deep into our hearts. It's *all His!*

Many people are consumed with ownership. We long for the day when we can stop renting and own a home. We take pride and satisfaction in owning certain cars, boats, or other large possessions. There is a sense of security in owning enough clothing, furniture, or home necessities. And yet, the reality is it's all on loan.

Psalm 24:1–2 clearly pronounces who owns everything: "The earth is the Lord's, and everything in it, the world, and all who live in it; for he founded it upon the seas and established it upon the waters."

Matthew 25 offers another look at God's view of ownership. In the parable of the talents, Jesus explains God's attitude toward money and our management of it. Jesus tells His listeners truths about the character of God and the kingdom of heaven through stories such as this one: A man goes on a journey and gives three servants different amounts of money, or talents, to care for while he is away. Each one does something different with the amount he is given. Two of them invest the money. One had five talents and gained five more. Another had two talents and gained two more. And one hid his one talent in the ground and gained nothing.

The two who had gained something were told the exact same thing: "Well done, good and faithful servant! You have been faithful with a few things; I will put you in charge of many things." But the third servant who hid the money entrusted to him was told, "You wicked, lazy servant! So you knew that I harvest where I have not sown and gather where I have not scattered seed? Well then, you should have put my money on deposit with the bankers, so that when I returned I would have received it back with interest" (Matthew 25:26–27).

Read carefully these words in the last sentence: "You should have put *my* money on deposit" (emphasis mine). Jesus is very clear about God's view of money and our responsibility. He's also clear about God's disappointment when we don't care for His money. I sure don't want God to call me wicked or lazy!

God desires for us to responsibly enjoy the gifts He gives. This Scripture passage shows God also watches to see how we manage His gifts. When we prove we are good stewards, He entrusts us with more. When we are poor stewards, He removes His possessions from our care. At the end of the parable of the talents we read this verse: "Take the talent from him and give it to the one who has the ten talents. For everyone who has will be given more, and he will have an abundance. Whoever does not have, even what he has will be taken from him" (Matthew 25:28–29).

We please God when we care for His money wisely. Creating and living by a budget is a great way to show God you care about being a faithful servant.

It helps us learn how to plan.

Budgeting involves planning, which is a godly attribute. Two of my driving goals in life are to become more like Jesus and to reflect God's character in all I do. Choosing to be intentional with money according to God's standard is one way to shape my character more like His.

God says this about His plans:

"Remember the former things, those of long ago; I am God, and there is no other; I am God, and there is none like me. I make known the end from the beginning, from ancient times, what is still to come. I say: My purpose will stand, and I will do all that I please. From the east I summon a bird of prey; from a far-off land, a man to fulfill my purpose. What I have said, that will I bring about; what I have planned, that will I do" (Isaiah 46:9–11).

God has plans for all of creation—everything, including us. Jeremiah 29:11 says, "'For I know the plans I have for you,' declares the LORD, 'plans to prosper you and not to harm you, plans to give you hope and a future.'"

Some might fear that making plans hinders what God wants to do. I believe that if we are seeking God's will, that if our hearts are right with Him, then He will direct our plans. Proverbs 19:21 reminds us that God is ultimately in control of our plans. "Many are the plans in a man's heart, but it is the LORD's purpose that prevails."

It frees us to serve God.

When we budget our money wisely, taking care to tithe, save, and stay out of debt, we open doors for God to use our resources and us. On the flip side, poor financial stewardship puts limits on us and can lead to disobedience.

With good stewardship, we have money to tithe and give offerings above the tithe. We have resources to help a family member or fellow believer in need. With sufficient savings, we can weather a financial storm without going into debt or taking a job that isn't in God's plan for us.

Debt is probably the most oppressive financial condition of all. With debt, you are in bondage to financial institutions. Instead of being available for God's use, your money is already spoken for. You end up being controlled by and serving your money, rather than serving God.

Jesus knew that the love of money could draw us away from God. In Matthew 6:24 Jesus said, "No one can serve two masters. Either he will hate the one and love the other, or he will be devoted to the one and despise the other. You cannot serve both God and Money."

Let me ask you a question. If you could do anything for God and knew you wouldn't fail, what would you do? I've asked this question of many women, and the dreams God puts in their hearts make mine soar. I've heard women say they'd love to open a house for unwed mothers, help the homeless find jobs, self-publish a book, or go on a mission trip. The most common restrictions on these dreams are fear and finances.

Imagine what God could do with a world full of financially wise Christians ready to serve Him, who aren't limited by debt, who have saved for a storm, and who have returned the ownership of their money to God.

It's critical for a fluctuating income.

A budget becomes increasingly important on a fluctuating income. If you plan to earn money by sales or starting a home-based business, you'll need to plan for the lean months.

A November 2004 online article entitled "Budgeting on a Fluctuating Income," Crown Financial Ministries (www.crown.org) offers this advice for families with an unpredictable income: "One way to assure that enough funds have been set aside to meet the monthly budget requirements is to deposit all income into a savings account. Then an average monthly salary can be withdrawn from that savings account, thus leveling out the months of high and low income."

It helps us to bring spending under control.

As you revise your budget to reflect your employment change, your first step should be to rein in your spending. To do that, you'll need to determine where you spend more than you should. Many of us have trouble with this because our spending becomes a blur. Getting to the root of the issues takes careful tracking.

Years ago when I first went to Weight Watchers, we tracked food eating habits according to specific food groups. All food was assigned a point value based on serving size and other factors. Then, we were allowed a certain number of points in areas like dairy, protein, and carbohydrates. While I don't remember the specifics, I know that on most days I had hit the maximum amount of carbs by 10:00 in the morning. Obviously that was, and continues to be, a problem area for me.

It took recording everything I ate to figure out why I wasn't losing weight. It's the same with spending. Sometimes it's just impossible to see how our purchases can add up to so much by the end of a month. But it silently slips past us, as we shop in ignorant bliss. Just as my weight continued to rise as I munched happily on tortillas and hot buttered rolls.

You might want to purchase a notebook or three-ring binder to keep track of your expenses. If you are computer savvy, there are programs like Excel that can help. Identify different areas of expenditures (use the list at the end of this chapter as a guide) and start recording your spending. If you do use a paper and pencil system, give yourself one piece of paper for each category.

After you've kept good records for a month or two, you'll see habits that can be changed. When you do, make a commitment before God to reduce your spending, especially in the areas that led you into debt.

It helps us to pay off debt.

When my first son was born, I wanted to work part-time, but debt kept me from doing so. A big portion of my income paid for the two new cars we drove. The problem was obvious. My husband and I drastically slashed our spending and focused all extra income on paying off the vehicles. Within a year, I started working less.

Unfortunately, so many Americans live backwards. Instead of saving, paying, and then acquiring the product, we acquire, then pay, with no margin for saving. Our grandparents didn't live this way. Our generation is under the dominion of debt. But debt isn't God's best for anyone.

Cardweb.com, Inc., is an online company that tracks and publishes information pertaining to all types of payment cards. Their studies contend that 80 percent of US households have at least one credit card. Of those families, the average debt was $8,940 in 2002 and climbing. This is not God's plan for His children.

Paul writes in Romans 13:7–8, "Give everyone what you owe him: If you owe taxes, pay taxes; if revenue, then revenue; if respect, then respect; if honor, then honor. Let no debt remain outstanding, except the continuing debt to love one another, for he who loves his fellowman has fulfilled the law." According to this Scripture passage, the only debt we should have is to love each other.

Debt wasn't acquired overnight, and it won't go away quickly. Paying off debt is a long-term commitment. Most financial experts suggest making a list of all your debts and start paying more than the minimum due on the smallest one. When that's paid off, start paying off the next smallest, and so on. If debt is your habit, it will take a change of thinking and spending to live debt-free.

Develop Good Spending Habits
Learn to distinguish wants from needs.

My friends Len and Deborah Ehrfurth are lay financial counselors and part of the Transition Home ministry team as our biblical budgeting advisors. In fact, Deborah has written an outstanding 365-day devotional called *Meditations on Money*. In their many years of counseling, the Ehrfurths have seen countless families floundering financially. They've found one of the biggest reasons to be the confusion between wants and needs.

Deborah says, "The vast majority of second incomes are not for needs, but for wants. This is because people commonly 'justify' their wants as needs. The big three needs are food, clothing and shelter, but in an affluent society like ours, we tend to interpret these on a much grander scale. Food becomes eating out frequently; clothing becomes the latest fashions; and shelter is not a modest home in a decent neighborhood but a showplace in a new subdivision."

Change your decision-making criteria.

Len and Deborah also advise changing our decision-making practices. In the Transition Home seminars, they challenge us to consider if we serve "mammon" (meaning wealth or riches) or God in our financial decisions. The question is raised, Do we buy a house because our money tells us we can afford the payments, or because God led us to buy that house?

This shift in reasoning is profound. It calls us to seek God's will in this area of our lives and to account daily for our spending decisions before the Lord. It's a good discipline to wait upon God for direction when buying certain items. Most of the time, we can wait before buying. While waiting, God might reveal other options or He might confirm the purchase. Asking God trains us to depend upon Him and helps develop self-discipline, which is always needed in the area of finances.

Practice self-discipline.

Self-discipline is often unpleasant because it involves restraint and dying to some selfish desire. Exercise is good for me, but I'd rather relax. Vegetables are healthy, but I'd rather eat lasagna. A small portion of food is enough, but I'd rather nibble on my kids' leftovers. I fight an ongoing pull towards self-indulgence each day.

Many women experience a similar battle with spending. There is pleasure in purchasing a new outfit, shoes, or home accessory. Some describe it as a high. For some, this is a minor problem and can be conquered easily. But for others, overspending could be a sin for them. When that's the case, they are catapulted into a spiritual battle to control their spending.

Kelley Reep, in her article "The Dieting Battle" in the June 2006 issue of *P31 Woman* magazine, makes an astute observation about our desires: "I now see that my expectations came from a misunderstanding of what it means to be "dead to sin" (Romans 6:11). I thought that being dead to sin meant having no *desire* to sin. But that's not the meaning of the text. The verb tense establishes our death to sin as a completed task; it is not something *you* complete through your effort. It is not a death to *desire*; rather, it is a death to *dominion*. That is, we have died to the rule of sin and are under no obligation to obey it any longer."

Through God's power, each of us is able to practice self-discipline in our spending. Through prayer and soaking our minds with biblical truths about money we can turn the focus off gratifying our desires and onto a self-disciplined life. I recommend identifying some Scriptures about money and memorizing them. Deborah Ehrfurth's book *Meditations on Money* is another tool you can use.

Proverbs 13:18 tells us, "He who ignores discipline comes to poverty and shame, but whoever heeds correction is honored."

Budget Expenses

You are now ready to create a workable budget. This doesn't have to be fancy or complicated. Just follow some simple guidelines and you are ready to create a budget. You should probably create two budgets: one for now and one for when you transition home. That way, you can start making changes to pave the way home. The process is the same for both.

Step 1: Identify your gross monthly income.

Although most of us think the amount on our paycheck is our income, that's not the case. It's better to identify our gross income and subtract from there. That way, if you become self-employed, you'll be used to thinking about items like medical insurance, state and local taxes, and FICA as customary expenses.

Step 2: List actual or anticipated expenses in various categories.

First identify those you know stay the same each month, like your tithe and mortgage. For those that fluctuate monthly (like utilities and gasoline), add your bills for the past year and divide by 12. If you don't keep your bills, make an educated guess. I've included some possible categories with individual line-item expenses at the end of the chapter.

Step 3: Plan for the budget busters that happen infrequently.

Examples could be your automobile license renewal, car repairs, or your home repairs. Perhaps you have some annual dues or renewals. Estimate when necessary and add up those items. Then divide by 12 to get your monthly set-aside amount.

Step 4: Assign spending guidelines for each category.

One guideline is the 10/10/80 plan. Allocate 10 percent of your gross income to your tithe, 10 percent to savings, and live on the balance. If saving 10 percent of your income is impossible now, then pick a smaller amount and work your way up.

Larry Burkett's book *Women Leaving the Marketplace* (Moody Publishers, 1995, reprinted with permission) offers another guideline for assigning a certain percentage of your income to specific categories. You'll notice he bases the percentage for the tithe and taxes out of your gross income. The other percentages are based on your net income. Here are Larry Burkett's recommendations:

Tithe	10% of gross
Taxes	15.5% of gross
Housing	38% of net
Food	12% of net
Auto	15% of net
Insurance	5% of net
Debts	5% of net
Entertainment and Recreation	5% of net
Clothing	5% of net
Savings	5% of net
Medical	5% of net
Miscellaneous	5% of net
School/Child Care	8% of net*

*Child care is not included in the 100 percent. If this is an expense for you, then subtract 8 percent from other categories.

Of course, you'll need to assign percentage guidelines that work for your family. This is just a place to start.

Step 5: Prepare to revise.

Don't be surprised if you need to revise your budget for a few months. You may find you don't need as many new clothes as you thought, or you really can spend less by using the slow cooker. Give yourself the flexibility to adapt when needed.

Preparing a budget isn't the hard part. Keeping a budget is really the challenge. As you prepare to leave the workplace, or if you are already home, may God give you the strength and wisdom to make wise financial decisions that honor Him and bring peace to your life.

Possible Budget Categories

Housing and Utilities

- Mortgage payment or rent
- Homeowner's insurance
- Property taxes
- Homeowner's association dues
- Electricity
- Water
- Garbage pickups
- Natural gas

Household

- Groceries
- Laundry
- Towels and linens
- Home improvement projects
- Cleaning supplies
- Dry cleaning
- Clothing

Transportation

- Car payments
- Gas
- Repairs
- Rental cars
- Insurance
- Routine maintenance
- Air travel
- Public transportation

Entertainment

- Cable TV or satellite service
- Internet access
- Sporting events
- Dining out
- Lessons and recitals
- Movies or shows

Communication

- Telephone
- Cellular phone

Health/Beauty

- Haircuts, perms, etc.
- Makeup
- Weight loss
- Nutritional supplements
- Medical, dental, and vision expenses

Debts

- Credit card payments
- Other loan payments

Pet Care

- Grooming
- Training
- Food

Other

- Child care
- Allowances for children
- Books, magazines, music
- Fast food
- Investments
- Vacation
- Spending money
- Children's sports activities
- Gifts (Christmas, birthdays, anniversary, etc.)

CHAPTER 6
• • • • • • • •

CREATING A TRANSITION PLAN

M y son spent an enjoyable Sunday afternoon at a friend's house. I chatted with his mother, Jenny, while waiting for shoes and balls to be gathered. Jenny is a teacher at my children's school and had become a friend.

"What are you doing this afternoon?" I asked.

"Laundry," she answered, breathing a weary sigh.

"That's what I'm doing tomorrow," I countered, commiserating in a way only another mother can.

"You're lucky. I wish I could stay home like you," Jenny answered.

"I know," I agreed, "I'm very thankful to be at home."

I've thought about her comment many times since that day. It broke my heart to hear the longing in her voice. She wanted to be at home. But I couldn't agree with her assessment of my situation. Luck had nothing to do with it. I didn't wake up one day to find my debts were paid off or to suddenly discover my family could live on one income. That didn't take luck; it took planning and a lot of hard work—and it took believing in and acting upon God's call.

If God is calling you to transition out of the workplace, you need to know that it can be done. It may not be easy, but it will be worth it. It will probably involve sacrificing something, but the benefits will far outweigh the temporary discomfort that accompanies change.

For years, my husband and I lived the "typical" American life. We both enjoyed our careers, drove new cars, and lived in an average neighborhood. With student loans, home expenses, and three children, we found ourselves with growing debt.

There are many areas in life where it is desirable to be above average. But being in debt is not one of them. When my husband and I would hear reports of the average debt for an American family, we would look at each other and jokingly say, "Well, at least we are above average."

It wasn't very funny because financial obligations controlled our lives and affected our ability to follow God's will. With all our money tied up in paying bills, there was little discretionary income. We weren't even tithing. We felt as though we were caught in a spider's web that was binding us to this progressively limiting lifestyle of work and debt.

When I knew God wanted me to work from home, my husband and I took a hard look at our circumstances and knew we needed to make changes.

There are two ways to approach a situation such as this. Taking a victim mentality is one way. The other way is to have faith that if God is calling you into the home, then He will make a path. Your part is to walk that path and make the tough decisions needed to not veer.

Unless you receive a windfall, you, like most people, will need a financial plan for transitioning out of the workplace. This plan needs to include paying off debts and creating a livable one-income budget. If it's not possible to live on one income, then the plan should include replacing income with work from home.

Five Steps to Creating a Transition Plan
Step 1: Cover your plan in prayer.

Scripture is clear that a battle exists. But it is not a battle of flesh and blood; instead it's a battle for our minds. As you step out in faith, obeying God's call to leave your dependable working environment and work from home, expect some spiritual warfare. It would be naive to proceed doing the work of God without a basic understanding that Satan hates what we are doing, will attack us in our weakest areas, and doesn't play fair. We can't afford to underestimate our enemy. Satan knows our past, he knows our vulnerabilities, and he will use those against us when he can.

The Deceiver will whisper lies in your ear: *"You'll never make it; your God won't provide for your financial needs; you'll go crawling back to your employer—just you wait and see. You aren't good enough, smart enough, skilled enough."* And on and on he goes.

When the doubt starts growing, we have two choices. The first is to believe the lies and admit defeat before we ever start. The second is to trust that if God has called us, then He will equip us. You see, God says something completely different about you. He says you have value and potential. He loves you enough to have chosen you from among all people to be His beloved.

First Peter 2:9 says, "But you are a chosen people, a royal priesthood, a holy nation, a people belonging to God, that you may declare the praises of him who called you out of darkness into his wonderful light."

As part of your preparation for leaving the workplace, consider preparing your mind for the impending battle. Based on the precept that a thief cannot enter a well-guarded home, your personal life must be covered in prayer. In Ephesians 6:10–11, Paul tells the believers how to protect themselves. "Finally, be strong in the Lord and in His mighty power. Put on the full armor of God so that you can take your stand against the devil's schemes." The chapter goes on to describe the famous picture of putting on the armor of God and culminates in verse 18 with the request to "pray in the Spirit on all occasions with all kinds of prayers and requests. With this in mind, be alert and always keep on praying for all the saints."

As we boldly follow God into this next phase of our lives, we are a bit like warriors. We need "weapons of warfare" that have the power to overcome fear and doubt. Please begin to pray now before you go on to step 2 of creating a transition plan. Without the "divinely powerful" prayer coverage, Satan could start his "lie attack" as you evaluate your current financial situation.

Step 2: Begin tithing.

If you have never tithed before, now is the time to start. Tithing is simply giving God a portion of what He has already given you. Although this advice may seem impossible given the fact that you are trying to *reduce* your expenses, Scripture is clear this in one of the first acts of obedience for a believer.

Malachi 3:10 instructs us to take the first tenth of our incomes and to put it in the "storehouse," which is the local church:

"Bring the whole tithe into the storehouse, that there may be food in my house. Test me in this," says the Lord Almighty, "and see if I will not open the floodgates of heaven and pour out so much blessing that you will not have room for it."

This act of obedience is the only one in which God says "test me." When you align your finances with God's will, there is a promise of blessings that will overflow.

The other side of the coin is what happens when we don't tithe. In the verses before verse 10, the Lord is speaking to the Israelites:

"I the Lord do not change. So you, O descendants of Jacob, are not destroyed. Ever since the time of your forefathers you have turned away from my decrees and have not kept them. Return to me, and I will return to you," says the Lord Almighty.

"But you ask, 'How are we to return?'

"Will a man rob God? Yet you rob me.

"But you ask, 'How do we rob you?'

"In tithes and offerings. You are under a curse—the whole nation of you—because you are robbing me" (Malachi 3:6–9).

I don't know about you, but I cringe when reading those words. I'd sure like to explain that passage away by saying it was meant for just the Israelites at that specific time in history. Except the opening words nix that excuse—"I the LORD do not change." Yes, we are under grace. Yes, the Lord forgives our sin. But we need to turn from disobedience with a repentant heart.

It would be remiss of me to avoid this important yet uncomfortable topic. And yet, I believe God wants to bless you in all ways as you transition out of the workplace. Being obedient with your giving is integral.

Step 3: Set a realistic goal to start working at home.

There are many variables that come into play when setting a goal to start working at home. It will depend on your current debt, how much money you need to make, and how you want to make it (i.e., telecommuting, direct-sales business, or home-based business from scratch). For instance, if you will start telecommuting for your current employer and in your current position, you might be able to start in a few weeks. If you need to research options for making money, then give yourself some time.

Once you've set a realistic goal date, write it down and post it in clear view. Then, make a list of everything you need to do before that date and start chipping away at it.

Step 4: Pay off debt and reduce expenses.

The next step in the transition plan is to pay off debts while reducing expenses, as discussed in the budgeting chapter. You'll want to start working at home with the best possible financial condition.

Look at every item on your budget and be ruthless. Make easy changes first such as eating at home instead of at restaurants, ironing your own work shirts, and shopping at secondhand stores. Some expenses may seem too little to bother with, but they quickly add up.

Then consider more difficult changes like selling a new truck that guzzles gas and buying an inexpensive smaller car. Maybe sell a boat or a camper. You might even need to move into a more affordable home or apartment.

Step 5: Start working from home before you quit.

If possible, start researching different opportunities and begin working from home before you quit your job. This extra money can pay off your debt, or you can begin to save. If you do start your own business before resigning from your current position, be very careful not to do any personal business on company time. Also, don't in any way undermine your employer by soliciting the company's customers as your future customers while still employed. These are unethical business practices and could lead to a lawsuit in the future—not to mention the danger of being terminated before you resign.

One benefit of finding work from home before you transition is that you can try different jobs without worrying about the income. Chapters 8, 9, and 10 outline in greater detail different options for working from home.

A Transition Plan for Singles

Can a single woman, with or without children, work from home? Absolutely! The transition plan is exactly the same as for a married individual, with one exception: Without the cushion of another income, you'll need to completely replace your income before you resign.

Lynda Evans is a perfect example of a single mom who determined to overcome her difficult situation and fulfill her dream of working from home.

In 1993, Lynda's husband of 20 years requested a divorce. While their marriage wasn't storybook perfect, it certainly didn't warrant a divorce, at least not in Lynda's mind. The news crushed Lynda. Rejection and depression flooded her heart and spirit. The smallest victims, Lynda's children, eight-year-old Brittney and five-year-old Jenna, were heartbroken.

The divorce process dragged on for 3 painful years while Lynda hoped her husband would change his mind. He didn't. In 1996 it was final; Lynda was on her own with two little girls.

Lynda was thankful to have a successful career as a grade school teacher. This was a wonderful source of income and security during the tumultuous divorce. Because the girls attended school where Lynda taught, she was able to manage the difficulty of scheduling alone. Although life ran smoothly on the surface, the undercurrent was rough.

Still struggling with depression and feelings of failure, Lynda labored through each week. The girls were angry and resentful, often responding with violent outbursts. By the end of the school day, Lynda was physically and emotionally drained by the demands of the children she taught.

Lynda remembers well the day she'd had enough. She recounts: "About a year after the divorce, one day at school I was standing out on the playground watching all these kids running around being happy and having fun, and I knew my kids were hurting deep inside. I just said to myself, 'I'm not happy, my kids aren't happy, I want to be home and not be here anymore.'"

Without an obvious and immediate way out of her situation, Lynda began investigating her long-term options. Her brother presented one opportunity. At that time, he was involved in a home-based Internet business and said exactly what she needed to hear. "You need to take a look at this—it's a way you can come home." Lynda checked out the company, joined a team of other committed adults, and began her journey home.

It took 3 years of hard work before Lynda was able to quit her teaching job and work from home full-time. During those 3 years, Lynda and her daughters became a team. Lynda chose to homeschool the girls, and all three of them grew as individuals and as Christians. Although Lynda had accepted Jesus as her Savior before her divorce, it was during the darkness of that time that she truly developed a relationship with Him. As the love of Christ transformed Lynda's personality and identity, her daughters shed their anger and resentment. The girls came to accept Jesus as their Lord at an early age, and together they matured in their faith.

Part of the reason it took 3 years to transition out of her teaching job was the internal battle that raged after Lynda's divorce. Lynda thought, "How can I be successful when I'm a leftover?" These and other negative beliefs had taken root in her mind, and the struggle of "you can/you can't" overwhelmed her at times. According to Lynda, "I had a self-image issue that was controlling me, until I learned to control it."

Single women have the challenge of not having another adult at home to offer daily encouragement. Lynda had to learn to motivate herself. Every day when she looks in the mirror, she focuses on her strengths, not weaknesses. If she doesn't, she gets discouraged.

To remain motivated while living out her dream of working from home, Lynda realized some life-changing truths that can apply to single or married women. First, she says, she had to change her frame of mind about who she was. All the negative labels she had given herself as a divorced woman peeled away as she learned her true identity in Christ.

"If you are going to change where you are, you have to change who you are and how you think," Lynda counsels. "I started reading books that would feed into me the truth about the seeds of greatness God placed inside me that needed to be nurtured and tended to. I read the Bible, listened to tapes, and associated with people that were helping me grow. I knew enough about God to know that He didn't want me to stay in the depth of sadness."

The second thing that kept Lynda going was to focus on the "why" of her transition. "I kept thinking about why I wanted to be home. I had a huge why and I had nothing to lose," she remembered.

As a result of this personal growth, Lynda's faith blossomed, her thinking changed, her understanding of her purpose developed, and her confidence exploded. Then, as a result of those changes and her association with her brother and his team, Lynda experienced a measure of success in her business. As she grew emotionally and professionally, she also developed a desire to help others grow, and she intentionally set out to develop her leadership skills. Lynda now oversees teams of people throughout the region and is helping others fulfill their dreams of being home. Brittney and Jenna are young women with a passionate love for Jesus, active in church, and are developing personal goals for their careers and home-based businesses.

Lynda's final advice for single women: Pursue your relationship with God and surround yourself with people who encourage you. You may think you are on your own, but you aren't. "The Lord is not just your confidant, He's the lover of your soul; when you go to bed at night He's the only one there and you constantly have to remember who you are in Him. Had I not had the Lord, I would not have had hope, and hope is what got me out of where I was," Lynda said.

It wasn't easy, but it was possible. Lynda loves to tell her story, certainly not to brag, but to encourage other single women who believe they can never be home.

Is There Another Way?

While this chapter outlines the "ideal" transition out of the workplace, reality is seldom cut and dried. A new mom's heart is breaking as she drops her baby at the sitter's, and decides she can't do this one more day. Your junior high daughter is getting into trouble after school and needs you home tomorrow. Your mom has a stroke and you become a caregiver. Sometimes, God just says, "Go." These situations happen every day. And when they do, creating a neat and tidy transition plan isn't an option.

When life is out of our control, we need to turn to the One who is in ultimate control. I believe God uses these times to train us to depend upon Him. I've found that when my plans have been derailed, when my life isn't going like I think it should, this is often when God's plan is made clear. Proverbs 19:21 speaks the truth, "Many are the plans in a man's heart, but it is the LORD's purpose that prevails."

If your transition out of the workplace wasn't as *you* planned it, perhaps God has got a great lesson in store. Trust that He will care for your needs and work it out for your good.

CHAPTER 7
· · · · · · · ·

DISCOVERING YOUR SKILL SET

At this point in your transition home, you have confirmed God's call on your life to do so, your eyes are open to the realities of working at home, and you have created a transition plan. Congratulations! This is a satisfying position because you are now better prepared than the majority of people leaving the workplace.

If you haven't already done so, the next step in the process is to identify how you are going to bring in the income needed to fulfill your budget requirements.

The options for making money are varied and numerous. An old-school thinking process might lead you to believe you'll need to sell makeup or storage containers. While those options are available, the vista for working at home has expanded exponentially in the past few years.

Home workers can choose between three major categories of employment:

1. Starting a home-based business (from scratch, purchasing an

existing business, or buying a franchise)

2. Investing in a direct-sell business (makeup, for example)

3. Telecommuting (for your existing company or a company that hires work-at-home employees)

Each employment opportunity requires a unique set of personal skills to be successful. For instance, if you love talking with people and developing relationships face-to-face, then a direct-sell business might be for you. If you would rather interact with your computer than a human, certain home-based businesses would work better. If talking on the phone makes your head ache, then don't go near some telemarketing jobs.

This chapter will set the stage for identifying what type of business is best for you. You'll be given the opportunity to assess your unique skills, your personality, and your desires for your life.

This is a critical step because many of us have lost sight of our dreams. I believe God gives us dreams for our lives, sometimes beginning when we are very young. Ask any child what she wants to be when she gets older, and she'll likely have an answer. Over time, the expectations of others or the unrealistic expectations of ourselves have shrouded those dreams, and often God's best for us.

Unfortunately, many women have grown up trying to fulfill someone else's expectations of them rather than God's. While still children, people start expecting us to do things we weren't created to do and it's a struggle to release the roles others assigned us.

A Role Not Meant for Us

I grew up a freckle-faced brunette in a neighborhood of blondes—13 of them. Not just any blonde, but the light, almost white kind of blonde. To say I stood out in the crowd was an understatement. Normally it didn't matter to any of us, except when we played "The Big Valley."

In the late 1960s, *The Big Valley* was a popular television show. For those of you over 40, you're humming the theme song right now. . . . "The big valley, the big valley . . ." (OK, I know there weren't any words). As little kids we would reenact the various episodes and, inevitably, there was an argument over who would get to play Audra Barkley.

Audra was the beautiful long-haired daughter, fussed over by her mama and pampered by her three handsome brothers. As much as I would have liked to have played Audra, that was never an option. You see, Audra had long blonde hair. With my brown hair, I wasn't even considered for Audra. I did, however, get a part. I was Nick. Not Heath, the handsome younger brother. The one boy in the neighborhood—Johnny, with blond hair—got to play him. No, I played Nick—the hotheaded troublemaker.

When I didn't play Nick, I (gulp) played a horse. These are embarrassing facts of my childhood that I'm only now able to talk about. I would have made a great Audra!

Although I write that tongue in cheek, the truth is, it hurts to be relegated to a role that doesn't fit you, whatever age you are. What I love about God's kingdom here on earth is that we each get to play a part specifically designed for us as we serve God in all parts of our lives, including work.

Your Childhood Dreams Versus Reality

Take a step back in time and consider what dreams you had as a child. Were those dreams a seed God planted in your heart? Or were they childish musings? If not, what happened to those dreams? If you're like many women, your dreams got lost in the reality of life. We take a job we don't want because we need the money. We set aside our dreams for those of our children. Or we pursue something we think we want, only to find it didn't answer the longing in our hearts.

When I was young, I wanted to be a teacher. My father was a high school biology teacher and I loved helping him at night grading multiple-choice tests, entering figures into his grade book, and hearing him talk about his class projects over dinner.

As a young girl, even into my high school years, I loved being in school. In fact, I enjoyed the learning environment so much that I volunteered in my elementary school library to reshelve books just to extend my time there. I admired and loved my teachers and worked hard to earn their respect.

Time passed and somewhere along the line I lost my dream to teach. It's possible that my dad's growing frustration with teaching subconsciously soured my opinion or, more likely, my own fascination with the businesswoman persona took over. When it was time to declare a major, I chose public relations. It would give me the opportunity to write, which I loved, and I could just see myself carrying a briefcase, heels clicking down the hall on my way to an important business lunch.

I finished my degree and entered the field of public relations. I relished my time writing brochure and ad copy, press releases, and newsletters. I also loved the administrative part of organizing special events and planning a marketing campaign. But when the time came to contact the media or make cold calls with business leaders, I inwardly cringed. I wanted to be an assertive businesswoman, but I was never happy in that role. And consequently, I was never very successful in that aspect of my career. The truth is that while I'm confident, I'm not aggressive. While I could play the part, my heart wasn't in it. I shined at the behind-the-scenes work, but faded up front.

Accept your weaknesses.

Being a child of the women's lib era, I had to be gut honest with myself in admitting that I couldn't do everything I set my mind to, and that I actually had some weaknesses—and that was OK.

We weren't created to be good at everything. The Scriptures are very clear that the Holy Spirit gives each of us certain "gifts." We excel in life and ministry when we identify those talents and skills and surrender them to God for His use. Sometimes finding our gifts is a process of elimination because weaknesses are often more obvious than talents. We shouldn't consider ourselves a failure when we discover a weakness. We're just one step closer to discovering a strength.

As you consider what type of work you'll do at home, being honest about your weaknesses is very important. Your weaknesses can do one of three things:

1. Stop you completely from pursuing certain types of work. For instance, if you couldn't sell a raft to a drowning man— that's a no-brainer.
2. Alert you to areas you'll need help with. Many women find

the business side of working at home to be a challenge. We may love the creative or relational parts of our job, but struggle through the accounting and recordkeeping. If this is you, then you'll need to invest in a good computer program or develop a relationship with an accountant at the get-go. That weakness shouldn't stop you, but just inspire you to work smarter.

3. Identify an area you need to personally address. Sometimes we need to correct weaknesses that can hinder our success. One weakness many have is with organization. That's why women's magazines can run articles every month on this subject and keep readers happy. We need help organizing the overwhelming amount of information and paper that works its way into our lives. Unless you can afford to hire a personal assistant or professional organizer, you'll need to address this problem head-on.

Another reason to identify your weaknesses is that you want to be happy in what you do. If you choose work that emphasizes a weakness, you'll be miserable. I've always disliked talking on the phone. It's partly because I don't think very fast, and consequently my words come out jumbled or I say something I didn't mean. When the pressure's on to think quickly, I'm a nervous wreck. This is a weakness of mine I've acknowledged and it's one reason I'm a happy camper communicating with email.

Knowing some of my weaknesses has helped me steer clear of work that emphasizes them and has caused me to enhance those that are crucial to my success at home.

Celebrate your strengths.

Now on to the very good news: God has given you numerous personal strengths, talents, and skills you can tap into as you begin to work from home.

Making a transition out of the workplace as a Christian really is done differently. As Christians, we understand that everything we do, whether cleaning our home, driving a carpool, or running a home-based business, is offered as a service to our Lord. Paul encouraged the slaves of his day with these timeless words in

Colossians 3:23–24, "Whatever you do, work at it with all your heart, as working for the Lord, not for men, since you know that you will receive an inheritance from the Lord as a reward. It is the Lord Christ you are serving." So as we identify our strengths, it's important to realize they are from God, to be used for God.

When we offer our skills back to God, He fine-tunes them and increases them according to our faithfulness in using them. Also, our God-given talents aren't something we just use at church or in a ministry. They are skills we integrate into all areas of our lives, including our home-based career.

Fortunately, I was in a job where I could identify some strengths. I was able to do that based on feedback I received from others and on my success with certain efforts like event planning or organization.

However, not everyone is in a job where his or her strengths are identified and utilized. You may find yourself scratching your head and wondering what skills you have that will be helpful as you transition home. Your strengths may be buried under years of nonuse or misuse, but they are still there.

Personal strengths like verbal communication or organization are like muscles. They atrophy with rest and strengthen with use. The spiritual gifts given by the Holy Spirit like teaching or administration are given in seedling form. In order for them to grow in a healthy way, they need to be used under submission of the Holy Spirit. We can use them in our own power, but they are more effective when we acknowledge that God gave them to us for His use.

Another truth about our strengths is we often have to discover them ourselves. This may take some trial and error. One way to do this is to volunteer. Churches and nonprofit organizations are always in need of volunteers. This is a safe place to try something new and discover a strength you may have overlooked.

I also believe that through personal introspection and prayer, God will reveal your strengths to you. In James 1:5, God promises us wisdom, if we only ask: "If any of you lacks wisdom, he should ask God, who gives generously to all without finding fault, and it will be given to him."

The Fulfillment of a Dream

I want you to consider that in addition to using your strengths in this next stage of your life, that God might also be using your transition out of the workplace to fulfill some of your dreams.

My dream to teach got buried as my life took different turns and twists. But God never forgot it. Although I didn't pursue teaching as a career, God always brought teaching into my life. At first it was with senior high kids at church, and then children of all ages. Teaching kids at church was a constant in my life for many years.

However, God had something more in mind. As I started working from home as an editor, God opened a door for me to do public speaking through Proverbs 31 Ministries. Back then I would have rather gone to the dentist than to speak in public to adults. But long ago, I told God I would be obedient to His leading. So, when opportunities arose to speak to groups, I accepted them. It didn't take long to see that God was fulfilling my childhood dream to be a teacher through speaking. God continued to fulfill my dream to teach through writing. God is good!

What dream have you neglected? Whatever it is, I guarantee you, God hasn't forgotten it. He may not fulfill it in the way you expect, but perhaps it will be even better as you surrender your plans and offer them to God for His use.

What Type of Work Is Right for You?

It's very likely that you already have an idea of the type of work you'll do from home. But for those who are unsure, I encourage you to do a personal assessment.

Consider God as a master painter. He has colored your life with:

- your personality
- your likes and dislikes
- your talents
- your physical ability
- your learning style
- your bent towards being an introvert or extrovert
- your spiritual gifts—teaching, prayer, administration, and others

As you consider which type of home-based work is right for you, take a look at your uniqueness. Be honest in your evaluation of your weaknesses and strengths. The way you are designed is just perfect for the way God wants to use you. Unless you know exactly what you want to do from home, I recommend you take some time and complete a thorough personal evaluation. Here are some areas to consider:

1. List your professional skills and experience.
2. List your personal strengths, such as hard worker or self-disciplined. Include your spiritual gifts in this category.
3. List your personal weakness, such as unorganized or not internally motivated.

Once you've completed this assessment, you are prepared to consider the options. The rest of the chapter outlines some general qualifications for working at home and some qualifications for the different types of work available.

General Work-at-Home Qualifications

All home-based work involves some common personal qualifications, such as being:

- self-motivated
- able to make decisions easily
- focused
- an independent worker
- able to manage one's time
- organized

Telecommuting Qualifications

If you want to work for an employer in a telecommuting position, you'll need the following skills and equipment:

- All of the general skills listed above.
- Computer skills. Most telecommuting jobs will require a computer.
- High-speed or broadband Internet connection. It's likely you'll need to be on the phone and computer at the same time.
- Phone skills. For some jobs, you'll need a dedicated phone line, and possibly unlimited long-distance service.

- Effective communication skills. This need increases with the lack of face-to-face contact. You'll need to communicate your needs clearly and succinctly.
- Past business experience. Whether it's customer service, accounting, or teaching, your past business experience is a key to telecommuting.
- Ability to work a regular schedule. While there is flexibility in telecommuting, there are still exterior deadlines. It is possible you'll need to arrange child care.

Home-Based Business Qualifications

If you want to own your own business, here are some skills you'll need:

- All of the general work-at-home qualifications.
- Big-Picture thinking. You'll need the ability to see and manage all the components of your business.
- Financial skills. Even if you have professional help, you'll need to know the basics of business finances in order to provide your accountant with the right information.
- Leadership skills. Motivation to make your business work will be completely up to you. Leadership skills can be learned and will be useful in all areas of your life.
- Problem-solving skills. Being the operator of a business means you make the decisions and solve the problems as they arise. This is great for those who love being in charge. However, it could be a challenge if decision making is difficult for you.
- Strategic thinking. Businesses are changing entities. They need to constantly grow and respond to changes. A business owner should always consider how her business can stay healthy.
- Marketing/Sales. Marketing is a necessary component of any business. This scares a lot of people who think it involves hard selling. Because of its importance, this book contains an entire chapter devoted to marketing.
- Recognizable expertise in your field, if you choose to practice a profession out of your home.

These lists aren't comprehensive. Working at home will require more self-discipline than you thought you'd need, and will require you to learn new skills and constantly increase your knowledge base.

As you review the preceding lists, don't be discouraged if your experience and personal assessment are lacking some of the components. Your learning curve will just be steeper than other people's. Be prepared to invest more time and energy into preparing yourself for the reality of working at home.

CHAPTER 8

· · · · · · · ·

TELECOMMUTING

In the 1800s, the landscape of the American workplace changed. No longer did the majority of workplaces feature dirt floors or unplowed fields, nor did they close up shop due to the weather. With the advent of the Industrial Revolution, many American workers moved from the fields to the factories. The workday no longer revolved around the rising and setting of the sun. Hot homemade lunches gave way to cold sandwiches in tin boxes as Americans gave up work done at home for factory jobs.

The Industrial Revolution actually began in England in the 1700s with the invention of steam power. This new source of energy enabled work previously done by family members, such as spinning yarn, to be completed more efficiently in mills and factories. Work done with hand tools was now done with machines, and the demand decreased for skilled workers. Cities grew where farms once thrived.

The changes wrought by the Industrial Revolution were far-reaching, and they still affect us today. Author Richard Hooker wrote this astute observation on the Washington State University Web site:

What drove the industrial revolution were profound social changes, as Europe moved from a primarily agricultural and rural economy to a capitalist and urban economy, from a household, family-based economy to an industry-based economy. This required rethinking social obligations and the structure of the family; the abandonment of the family economy, for instance, was the most dramatic change to the structure of the family that Europe had ever undergone—and we're still struggling with these changes.

Researchers say we are in a new age: the age of information. This era in history can roughly be traced to the invention of Samuel Morse's original telegraph transmitter and receiver in 1837. Of course, we enjoy the products of this new age, and can hardly remember a time when we didn't have them.

As we move deeper into the age of information, society is responding to the technological changes, and the pendulum is swinging. We are now seeing waves of American workers returning home. The reasons for this shift are varied and range from a desire for a slower life, need to care for loved ones, or a concern for the environment.

While reasons for working at home may differ, the mode for being able to do it is the same: the advance and affordability of technology. What a change two decades has wrought! In the early 1980s the jump from an IBM Selectric typewriter to the word processor was huge. Who could have imagined then the unbelievable quality and depth of work we can now do from home?

What Is Telework?

Because I'm on staff with Proverbs 31, a national women's ministry, but I don't work at their headquarters in Charlotte, North Carolina, I'm officially considered a teleworker or telecommuter. Each month I receive a paycheck, I have a boss, and I'm accountable to the ministry for the quality and timeliness of my work.

As the editor for the ministry's magazine, I interact with my home office, and I work with a graphic designer in Greensboro, North Carolina; a printer in Birmingham, Alabama; and with proofreaders, editors, and authors around the world. And I'm able to do this through the Internet and with a minimal investment in equipment.

A teleworker by the most common and broad definition is employed by a company. He or she may be paid as an employee or as an independent contractor—but is not self-employed. The benefits for this type of at-home work are many.

Benefits of Telework

I absolutely love my job and it would have taken me years to achieve this senior editing position and the opportunities it affords on my own. I'm thankful for the steady income, for being a part of a team of other teleworkers, and for having a great office support staff. Although I work alone, I never feel alone. My co-workers are just a phone call or email away. To combat isolation, I have developed a network of friends with similar working situations or who aren't employed. Being involved in a small group of Christian women writers helps keep me connected to others as I pursue my craft of writing.

Additionally, being part of an established ministry (or company) has opened doors for me professionally that would have been otherwise closed. My staff position at Proverbs 31 Ministries identifies me with a known entity and is a platform to expand my skills.

These benefits are why millions of Americans work some part of their workweek at home. Statistics vary depending on the definition of telework, but somewhere between 20 and 40 million employed workers are based at home.

The benefits to employees are obvious, with greater flexibility in their schedules being close to the top of the list. More flexibility is a direct lead-in to greater balance between work and family life. Most teleworkers can go on school field trips, take kids to football practice, have lunch with a spouse, or care for aging parents without worrying about accounting for every minute of time.

A huge bonus in telecommuting is the savings in time previously spent getting ready for work and commuting. For most people that adds up to at least five to ten hours a week, more if you live a distance from your workplace. Consider the cost of gas, and the savings are multiplied.

Another benefit of telecommuting is accountability. A telecommuting job is like any other job. You have a boss who monitors your productivity. This is great exterior motivation for those who benefit from structure.

Our health and our families' health can also improve. No more sending sick kids to day care or dragging ourselves into the office when we're sick, thereby infecting everyone with whom we interact! And the list of benefits goes on.

Not only do employees benefit from telecommuting, but employers do too. A study by the Employment Policy Foundation reported in the March 2004 issue of *Business & Legal Reports* stated the following:

The study found that the benefits of telework also extend to employers. Not only do teleworkers feel more productive, but the study found they actually are. The analysis cites a study of employees that found teleworkers handled 26 percent more calls and brought in 43 percent more business than workers doing the same job in the office. Additionally, the study found that teleworkers have lower rates of absenteeism and turnover.

Disadvantages of Telework
On the surface, it would seem that telework offers the best of all worlds: a great job, flexible hours, and close connection with home and family. What could possibly be wrong with this ideal situation? As with most great opportunities, there's a downside. I share some of the challenges of telework not to deter you, but to prepare you for possible hurdles. The best way to deal with hurdles is to be able to soar, not trip, over them.

You may feel isolated from your co-workers.
An obvious challenge in telework is isolation. This challenge

applies to anyone who works from home, whether telecommuting or self-employed in a home-based business. For a telecommuter, however, isolation from co-workers adds a distinct hardship.

Depending on your relationship with co-workers and your dependence upon them to complete your work, you'll need to get creative in maintaining connections with your company. You may find that others resent your position at home, or are afraid to "bother" you. In these instances, you must take the initiative to show your co-workers you value and need their input and that you welcome their calls. The burden does lie on you to maintain those important relationships with other employees.

In addition to ongoing work-related communication, make a point to remember special events in their lives such as birthdays and anniversaries. If you wait for others to remember you, you'll be disappointed and resentment could grow. Guard against it by making the first move.

You may develop mental myopia.

Another hurdle is the tendency towards myopic thinking. This is an ongoing challenge for me as an editor. Without input from others, I can easily slip into dangerous, narrow pathways. An isolated mind can drift into believing that everyone thinks the same—in other words, like me—and that's the way it should be! To avoid that, I intentionally ask others for their opinions on articles. I'm aware that by being isolated I can push my own agenda, which isn't good for the ministry or for the readers of the magazine. While I may be able to perform my job completely alone, I'm acutely aware of my need for others to bring balance and completeness to the end product.

This is an important concept for a Christian because we know that we are each created uniquely by God and given specific skills and talents at birth. Those of us who have accepted Jesus as our Savior are indwelled by the Holy Spirit, who develops those skills for the glory of God. Those who haven't yet accepted Jesus still have unique gifts, but operate in their own power, not God's.

This means that others have skills and talents that I don't. It takes wisdom to discern when others are more gifted in certain areas than I am. And at times it takes humility to ask for help. By affirming the skills and talents of others, they benefit through the affirmation. A double blessing is that we benefit when they share their skills with us. Telecommuters need to pursue relationships with others who are talented in other ways.

You may be tempted by distractions.

When I worked outside the home, each morning I firmly shut the door behind me and got in my car. It didn't matter what the kitchen, family room, kids' rooms, or my bedroom looked like—I couldn't see them anymore. My family and friends knew I worked and only called in case of emergency. I never watched daytime television, so it didn't matter what was on. If people called the house, they got the answering machine, which I checked at night.

Everything's different now.

Now I walk past dirty breakfast dishes to my desk. From my desk, when the light shines just right through the blinds, I can see a fine layer of dust on the table. Friends, relatives, and acquaintances know I'm home during the day and they sometimes call me. I know when my favorite cooking show is on, and I love watching the morning news. Distractions such as these can derail me from my work in a flash.

Although distractions existed when I worked outside my home, they were momentary and normally involved work. Now my distractions have the potential to pull me firmly away from work for hours, and in some cases, the rest of the day. Don't underestimate their potential danger when working at home.

I've found the secret to dealing with distractions is to prioritize what's important. For instance, it's important to me to have the kitchen clean and clutter free. That's easy to deal with. Another priority is for friends to feel welcome. I lived life for too many years with a "don't-bother-me" approach to interruptions. When the Lord convicted me of my attitude, I set about finding a balance to the needs of friends and family and my need to get things done. With Jesus as my role model, I'm learning how to welcome interruptions and to be more attuned to the times when I need to set aside my daily to-do list for God's.

Instead of letting the distractions of daily living frustrate you, be proactive. Spend some time thinking through what bothers you most and plan to address those issues one by one. Speaking bluntly and honestly, I must admit that children can be a source of frustration. Instead of being the reason we do what we do, they become the reason we can't get anything done. Depending on the age of your children, they will be limited in understanding that you are working. Consider this as an opportunity for training, work around their schedules, or get help. We'll discuss this concern in detail in another chapter, but it's enough for now to realize kids will distract you from work. My admonition is to expect it and prepare for it now.

You may find yourself becoming a workaholic.

If you thought the lines between work and home were blurred before, hold on to your fuzzy house slippers. A teleworker will go in one of two directions regarding work. The first is towards slothfulness. With no boss looking over your shoulder, and without a strong work ethic, it might be easy for your breakfast to slip into your morning coffee break, then a soap opera/ESPN, lunch, a Starbucks trip, a stop by the store and then, suddenly, wow, look at that, it's almost time to quit for the day. The good news is that slothfulness won't be a problem for long, as you likely won't have a job for long.

The second is towards workaholic tendencies. The lure to work just a bit more is always there—especially if your work area is in plain view. Like having a home-based business where the work never stops, teleworkers can feel they have to continually prove themselves. Without having a physical presence in the office to show they are working, they might feel the need to substantiate it with results.

Brad Schepp, author of *The Telecommuter's Handbook,* offers advice on dealing with the issue of workaholism, "One way to push aside these tendencies is to set goals for yourself. Meet them, certainly, but when they've been met, knock off for a while. You can always get back to it later."

If you know you tend toward working more than you should, then heed this advice. Set realistic goals for your morning, afternoon, day, or week. Review them at regular intervals to remind yourself of your progress and what needs to be done. Then discipline yourself to rest in the knowledge that you are accomplishing all you need to for that day. Many workaholics are uncomfortable with "white space" in their day. However, God needs us to have a somewhat open schedule for those "surprise" interruptions He's already got planned.

Where to Find Telecommuting Jobs

Telecommuting jobs can be found everywhere. They might seem a little like Easter eggs hidden in your backyard. You know they must be out there, but they aren't in plain view. There's not a telecommuting column in the newspaper want ads yet. The warnings against scams ring loudly in your ears. A friend's failed attempt at telecommuting is fresh in your mind. Are there legitimate telecommuting jobs to be had? Absolutely!

The trend toward companies hiring teleworkers is growing rapidly. Gil Gordon, telecommuting expert, predicts 10 to 15 percent annual growth in the number of telecommuters and an increasing diversity in the types of employers and job types involved. Telecommuting is somewhat like homeschooling, which was once on the fringe of society but now has a strong voice in the marketplace. Working at home, once done by a select group of workers, is becoming a viable alternative for employees at all levels.

With the dominance of knowledge-based work in the business world, those people with the knowledge can usually work anywhere given a computer, phone, and fax. Companies are adapting to this wave of worker and creating fair policies to do so.

Finding a quality telecommuting job will likely take more screening work on your part than a traditional job. This is because many telecommuting jobs aren't advertised as such. In fact, the employer might not even realize a job has the potential to be done at home. The Employment Policy Foundation report quoted previously in this chapter found that 65 percent of current jobs are amenable to telework. This means a telecommuting job could be right under your nose.

Start with your current employer.

The first place to start identifying a teleworking position is within your own company. In fact, it could be your current job. Ask yourself how much of your job could be done from home. Before you yell, "All of it!" and rush in to your boss's office with the good news, you should be prepared with a written proposal.

Your boss might not share your enthusiasm, and if that's the case, better to be armed with supporting information for why and how it could work.

A telecommuting proposal doesn't have to be a formal document, just an objective look at how you could do some, or all, of your job from home. Consultant Gil Gordon says the predominant attitude you are likely to encounter is skepticism, not rejection. So be prepared.

Your employer will want to know this move will benefit the company, so be careful not to list how it benefits you—that's obvious. Here are some common employer benefits you might include in your proposal:

- Increased productivity. You might outline the different distractions you face at your job. This might be time lost due to common interruptions (phones, salespeople), commuting issues, or challenging work environments (loud, cold). This point could either work in your favor if you are a strong employee or work against you if you have a history of whining. Blaming others or situations for our lack of productivity doesn't get anyone very far.
- Reduced need for office space. Depending on your employer's needs, your office and parking space may be a high premium. Include this in your proposal if it is.
- Reduced employee costs. Every employer spends money for miscellaneous expenses to office an employee. Normally, home workers assume the cost for office products, which could add up over time. This is a detail you would work out

with your employer. In addition to the small expenses which add up, there's no doubt your sick days would decrease. That's a big benefit to an employer. The State of California hired Fleming LTD to assess the savings of telecommuting employees. They arrived at an annual saving of $8,000 per employee! This didn't even include the savings on sick days.

- Retaining a knowledgeable employee. If you are a valued and knowledgeable employee, your company will benefit by retaining you. If you know training costs for new employees, here would be a great place to include them.

In addition to the benefits, offer practical information on how you'll approach different aspects of your job. Your thoroughness will show your employer this isn't an off-the-cuff idea.

If your current job doesn't lend itself to telecommuting and you have a good history with your company, consider changing positions. Approach this new position with the same type of proposal. If you aren't familiar with the position, be diligent in your research. Also, be open to the idea that you might have to work in the office for a while before transitioning home.

Before you ever approach your employer about telecommuting, be prepared for the answer to be no. Some employers just aren't open to the idea. A realtor friend tried to explain to her boss the benefits of working from home, but he just didn't buy it. He wants to see her face in the office every day.

If you meet with resistance, then suggest to your employer a trial basis. Offer to try it for three or six months. Of course, if it doesn't work out, then you'll need to reevaluate.

Put the Internet to good use.

Because almost all telecommuting jobs involve the Internet, you'll find most jobs through this avenue. However, some warnings are in order as you begin your search. First, a legitimate company will not ask you for any money up front. A telecommuting job is like any other job. There may be some requirements after you are hired, but if someone wants you to send a $50 application fee—run! Additionally, if they give you a 900 number to call, claim you'll make thousands in a week, say you don't need experience, or assert it's easy work, watch out. Those are common red flags you are about to get scammed. A true job will be presented as such.

There are two common approaches to finding a telecommuting job outside of your existing company. The first is a Web site that lists such jobs. One of the most popular is craigslist.org. This is a massive site that requires some digging on your part. Enter the type of work you want including keywords that indicate "telecommuting" or "work at home." Some common keywords include:

- telecommuting
- telecommute
- telework
- teleworking
- home-based
- home-based employee
- home-based employment
- home-based jobs

Other established Web sites that list current openings include:

- Christian Work at Home Moms (www.cwahm.com)
- Work at Home Moms (www.wahm.com)
- Telecommuting Moms (www.telecommutingmoms.com)
- Workaholics4Hire (www.workaholics4hire.com)

There are also legitimate organizations where you pay a fee to receive job listings. Two solid companies include Telework Recruiting (www.teleworkrecruiting.com) and Telecommuting Jobs (www.tjobs.com).

Other sources for job listings are companies that are known to hire teleworkers. The Transition Home Web site (www .transitionhome.org) maintains a current list of companies that are hiring. Telecommuting Moms also maintains a list.

Even with the best screening, scams can slip through the cracks. Be on the offensive and watch for suspicious clues.

Be proactive as well as reactive.
Contacting those companies who have posted an open position

is, of course, the most common job search technique. Lequetta Bramer, a professional recruiter and our Transition Home ministry expert in telecommuting, recommends an innovative approach to the telecommuting job hunt. She says this:

I strongly encourage those of you serious about seeking work at home, not only to be reactive to posted ads, but to also be proactive in sending your resume to employers who hire individuals with your skill set, even if they don't have an ad. Many employers will bring on additional staff should the perfectly qualified individual knock on their door. This is how I placed many professionals in my 10 years of recruiting accounting staff. It's also how I also obtained my current home-based market research recruiting position. I contacted one of the partners of the firm, told them my background, and expressed interest in working for their firm. Do some research, and find out who would hire someone with your background. You'll dramatically cut down on your competition this way.

How to Apply

Once you find a potential job, simply follow the employer's application procedures. Many will have you fill out an online application. Others will ask for a résumé. When that happens, put time and effort into creating a strong and descriptive résumé. In corporate America, a résumé gets your foot in the door, while a face-to-face interview seals the deal. In the telecommuting world, there will likely only be a phone interview. Consequently, your résumé needs to make a powerful first impression.

An added challenge for those seeking posted telework positions is that you are potentially competing with individuals across the country, not just those working in your city. Because of the competition, your résumé needs to be professional and stand out.

Here's an example of an ad for a real telecommuting position and the components you should include in your résumé.

Home-Based Call Center Agents
Canton Access, a leading provider of call center services using home-based customer service individuals, is looking for

enthusiastic agents to handle inbound customer calls. You must provide:

- Excellent customer service, communication, and relationship building skills.
- Previous customer service or sales experience required.
- Active listening and attention to detail with the ability to quickly organize and multitask in a fast-paced, changing environment.
- Strong computer and Internet skills.
- Ability to easily navigate through multiple screens.
- Passion, reliability, attention to detail, problem-solving skills, and the ability to multitask, work up to 20–35 hours. Ability to be self-motivated and successfully thrive in a work-at-home environment.

Résumé Components

As you put together your résumé to respond to this ad, be sure to include the following components.

Contact Information

List all the ways a potential employee can contact you. Triple check to make sure the phone number and email address are both correct.

Objective

This tells the employer which job you're applying for and, subtly, why you are right for that job. Unless you are applying for one type of job, such as customer service, this segment will change with each position. Make sure it matches the job listing. Pay close attention to the qualifications listed in the ad and make sure your objective indicates your desire for a position that would utilize your customer service skills.

- Example: To obtain an inbound customer service position where I can utilize my exceptional customer service and communication skills. *Do not include in your objective that you want to work from home.* This indicates to an employer that the position is secondary to being home.

Skills Summary

Although this advice sounds elementary, human resource professionals ask that you only apply when you have the requested qualifications. It's a waste of your time to do otherwise because you will be automatically disqualified.

A skills summary list can be bulleted. Use key words found in the ad itself or in ads for similar positions. Highlight your experience and skills, listing specific accomplishments. Many companies electronically scan résumés to find specific software or industry experience. Be sure to list these on your résumé, especially if they are included in the ad.

- Example: Ten years customer service experience; exceptional communication skills; strong computer and Internet skills; excellent attention to detail.

Education or Experience

The next items on your résumé should be your education and/or experience. List first which area is a greater qualifier for the position. If you have only recently graduated from college and have little work experience, then list your education before your experience. Most employers assume people have graduated from high school, so this would not be necessary on your résumé unless you have just graduated and have little work experience.

If you have years of experience in the related area, be sure to list this area first, then your educational background. It's important for the résumé reviewer to scan your résumé quickly and determine within a matter of seconds that you are worth a second glance.

Regarding your experience, be specific with your dates and excruciatingly honest with the details. Do not exaggerate your title or responsibilities, but don't downplay them either. If there are gaps in your history, a sentence or two of explanation might help.

References

Indicate they are available immediately upon request, and have letters of reference ready to fax, with current contact information for that reference.

Cover Letter

Always send your résumé with a separate cover letter. However, keep the letter short. Indicate why you are sending the company a résumé (how you heard of the job opening, or that you are interested in working for their firm). Include the most important skills and experience you would bring to their firm. Always focus on the benefit to their firm for hiring you and not what you want.

Telecommuting is a wonderful option for many people. In addition to being a worthwhile job opportunity on its own, it can also provide steady income while you pursue a home-based business. Depending on the job, telecommuting can provide a full-time income, equal to or greater than what you earned outside the home. Or it can provide spending money or pay for vacations. The possibilities are endless as technology advances and more businesses embrace the home-based worker.

CHAPTER 9
• • • • • • • •

HOME-BASED BUSINESS OPPORTUNITIES

My husband graduated from college with a degree in chemical engineering. Tod entered the environmental consulting field and for 20 years climbed his way up the corporate ladder. He worked for outstanding companies, learned about consulting and management, earned a master's in business administration that was paid for by his firm, and he oversaw employees. He worked diligently and was rewarded with a good salary, benefits, and great experience.

Because I worked from home, Tod was able to be flexible with his hours. He often left home at 6:00 in the morning, returned late, and traveled on a moment's notice. It was working well, except for the two aches in his heart.

The first ache concerned a dream he'd held for years to be his own boss. As with many employees, over the years he mused about the possibility, especially as his frustrations grew. Each time he was asked by his employer to lay off a good employee before Christmas, he'd think, "I would do this differently." While he could make many decisions, he didn't hold the ultimate authority.

The second ache concerned the time he wasn't spending with his family. We've learned, as most parents do, that as our children get older, they need our physical presence as much, if not more than when they were younger. Tod missed many sports practices, band and chorus concerts, and helping with homework. He never had lunch at school or went on a field trip. As our oldest son approached high school, Tod heard the clock ticking.

It was on a warm September morning as we sat on metal bleachers watching one of our boys play football when Tod brought up the idea of investing in some land. I couldn't imagine another loan payment in addition to our other expenses, and in frustration said, "If you want to invest in something, why don't you invest in yourself! Why don't you start that business you've been talking about for years?"

Now, mind you, I was thinking he might start something on the side while he kept his day job. But God was already working in Tod's heart and He had other plans. The idea took root and within a week we had a plan for Tod to transition out of the workplace and work from home full-time.

Within two months, we formed a limited liability company, Tod obtained professional liability insurance, we met with our personal insurance agent and got that in the works, pooled savings, and applied for a home equity loan to pay our bills until our business could support us.

Within five months of our September conversation, we started two home-based businesses. Tod opened a consulting business, and together we opened an online retailer selling cottage-style home and garden supplies. Our learning curve has been steep. While our professional backgrounds enable us to breeze through parts of our businesses, we struggle with others. We've learned a lot about our strengths. And, very importantly, we're learning when it's time to call in a specialist.

Within ten months, we were able to support our family with

home-based income. That is due in large part to having only a mortgage and one car payment when we started our businesses.

While it may be unusual to have both husband and wife at home in today's culture, we actually have joined a rich heritage of people who worked at home. In fact, at one time, almost every business was run from homes. As explained in the previous chapter, due to the Industrial Revolution, we saw a shift of work away from homes and to offices. The tide has changed not only for telecommuters, but also for business owners.

According to the Small Business Association, home-based businesses represent 52 percent of all firms in the country and provide 10 percent of the nationwide economy's total receipts. The research firm International Data Corporation reported that the number of home-based businesses was expected to eclipse 25 million by 2003. Nearly 8,500 new home businesses start every day, and there are no signs of a slowdown.

One dominant reason for the shift is the variety of options we have for making money at home. The previous chapter dealt with telecommuting, which involves working as a home-based employee. Since that's not for everyone, in this chapter, we'll look at the diversity of legitimate home-based business opportunities.

We'll take a look at the three main categories of home-based businesses:

1. Starting a home-based business from scratch
2. Investing in an established direct-sales or network marketing business
3. Purchasing a home-based business franchise

Before You Start
Ask yourself why.

Before you start down this entrepreneurial road, ask yourself this crucial question: Why do I want to start a home-based business? We are really good at answering the who, what, when, and where questions of life. But we often neglect the why.

When you can answer why you want to start a home-based business, you have greater focus and more motivation. David

Allen, author of *Getting Things Done,* writes, "To know and to be clear about the purpose of any activity are prime directives for clarity, creative development and cooperation. But it's common sense that's not commonly practiced, simply because it's so easy for us to create things, get caught up in the form of what we've created and let our connection with our real and primary intentions slip."

Your answer for why will be a useful tool when you get discouraged. If your answer to starting your own home-based business is why not, you'll get derailed quickly when the going gets tough. Also, if your answer has anything to do with running away from something you don't like, watch out. That's typically a weak reason. Make sure God is calling you to this new venture.

Change your thinking from employee to business owner.

From the moment you make your decision to be a business owner, you need to change your thinking. Lynda Evans, successful home-business entrepreneur, strongly advises:

"You can find the best business and the best product, but to be successful you will need to grow in new ways. You've been programmed all your life to think like an employee. You need to start listening to people who have successfully gone from point A to point B and started their own business."

This is a paradigm shift in how you approach your work. No longer will someone be setting goals and objectives for you—that's now your responsibility. Without this change in focus, you will waste lots of time through procrastination and insecurity. With the inception of your business, the mantle of leadership has been transferred to your shoulders. Embrace the change and start to think and act like a leader.

General Tips for Working from Home

As you change your thinking from employee to business owner, spend some time thinking through the professional side of the business. The relaxed atmosphere at home can be good and it can be bad. You'll want to implement some very professional practices at the beginning.

- Set up a good workstation. Even if you start out at the kitchen table, you'll need a plan. Chapter 14 focuses on practical tips for setting up your home office.
- Invest in good business cards and stationery. Hire a professional designer for this task. I know there are good computer programs on the market, but this is an area you don't want to skimp on. Lots of designers work at home, so you should be able to afford this expense. When you go to print, spend a few more dollars and use higher-quality paper.
- Prioritize your phone service. If you have others at home, consider getting a dedicated second phone line. That way you'll avoid a three-year-old telling your client that Mommy's in the bathroom right now. At the very least, train your children on proper phone etiquette and keep message pads by the phone.
- Set up boundaries for yourself at the beginning. As I did the research for this book and spoke with women working at home, this was a common thread of advice. Decide now when you will and won't work. Dedicate one day as your Sabbath rest and offer that day to the Lord. Trust Him to work out the details if it feels as if you are limiting your growth potential with this decision.

Starting a Home-Based Business from Scratch

This is the dream you have had for years. It could be assembling gift baskets, planning children's parties, or making and selling specialty cookies. This type of business almost always starts with your unique talents or experience.

If you have never owned a dog, never worked in a pet shop, and never had experience or instruction in obedience training, then you probably shouldn't start an animal behavior business. Just because you want to learn a skill doesn't mean you'll be successful at it. In other words, start with something you know.

You may have the perfect vision of the business you want to start. If not, the possibilities are almost endless. But how do you make a decision on what's right for you?

Janet Drez, author of *Putting the Pieces Together: A Christian Woman's Guide to a Successful Home-Based Business,* advises women on what type of home-based business to choose. She recommends asking yourself questions such as:

- What did you enjoy most about the last two positions you held?
- What did you like least?
- What did you study in high school or college that you enjoyed?
- What hobbies do you enjoy?
- What do your friends and family tell you you're good at?
- What are your family background and traditions?
- What are your spiritual gifts? (Romans 12:6–8, 1 Corinthians 12:7–11, and Ephesians 4:11 provide some lists to help you in answering this question.)
- What types of people do you enjoy being around?
- Do you need a business which is done mainly in your home (such as bookkeeping) or are you able to make appointments?
- If there were no limits or feasibility issues, what type of business do you think you'd like to start?
- Where would you like to be in two years in all areas of your life?

Armed with this information, you can proceed to brainstorm the variety of business opportunities available.

Here are some businesses that women have successfully run from home.

Special Event Businesses

Catering

Florist

Gift buying

Photography

Children's parties

Gift baskets

Party entertainment

Business to Business

Accounting/bookkeeping
Computer instruction/consulting
Executive recruiting
Foreign language translation
Personalized stationery
Public relations and marketing
Web site design/hosting

Family-/Children-Oriented Businesses

Baby proofing
Ballet/dance instructor
Cheerleading/Coaching/How to try out
Clothes recycling—children
Interior design for children's rooms
Etiquette for children
Memoir writing
Tutoring

Personal/Home Services

Art framing
Estate sale organizing
Image consulting
Miniblind cleaning
Seamstress

Cooking instruction
Home inspections
Jewelry
Travel agent

Reproduced with author's permission from Janet Drez, *Putting the Pieces Together: A Christian Woman's Guide to a Successful Home-Based Business* (Chandler, AZ: A Perfect Solution, 2000).

If you start a business from scratch, make sure your idea is marketable.

A word of caution as you brainstorm the wonderful possibilities for your business: Make sure other people will love the idea as much as you do. Otherwise you'll end up with lots of watermelon pickles, like my Uncle Will did.

My Uncle Will is a very creative and intelligent man. He enjoyed a successful career as a nuclear engineer and moved to a small farm in Kansas after his retirement. The entrepreneurial spirit has always surged through Will, and starting a home-based business was a natural fit for him.

In addition to his farm, he loves cooking, especially old recipes. Coming from a family of farmers, he had great memories of particular foods his grandmother made. One recipe involved the use of the watermelon rind to make pickles. Combining his desire for extra income with his love for his grandmother's watermelon pickles, Will set forth to start a business making and selling pickles.

Will went through all the proper channels and received the necessary health permits to prepare his product. He aptly named them Grandma's Watermelon Pickles and printed up cute labels. When his crop was ready, he clipped, cut, and cooked batches of the briny delicacy.

Unfortunately, his business didn't flourish. It seems the market was not quite ready for watermelon pickles. It's also possible that Uncle Will didn't find the right niche for his product. Or perhaps he should have offered five varieties of traditional pickles to offset the less popular watermelon variety.

The message in the story is this: Make sure there's a market for your service or product. Companies spend thousands of dollars on market research. McDonald's knows exactly where to put their golden arches, thanks to market research. But the normal small business owner doesn't have the funds and will need to be creative.

A tip for doing cheap market research is to look for trends in the marketplace. Perhaps Uncle Will could have assessed popular pickled items on a tour of farmer's markets in Kansas. For my husband and me, the launch of magazine *Cottage Living* fueled the opening of our cottage-style online retailer. What are trends in your area? What about specialty coffees? Every time I'm at my favorite Starbucks, I see professionals waiting in line. What if someone could offer a Starbucks office delivery service? I would have used it.

Another tip is to look for needs not currently being met. Paula Deen, restaurant owner and cooking show star, started her business from home selling boxed lunches to professionals in the area. The demand grew for her cooking, and Paula and her sons eventually opened a restaurant. Paula saw a need and met it. She succeeded beyond her wildest dreams by offering a quality product. What services do your co-workers and neighbors need and how can you meet it with quality?

My friend Karen sold advertising to small businesses. Her buoyant personality, creative ideas, and integrity made her very successful. As she interacted with customers, she realized that many small business owners needed a broader scope of marketing advice. Karen wanted to be home for her teenagers, so she started a marketing business specifically for small businesses who couldn't afford to hire an agency.

Put your team together.

The next step in being a successful home-based business owner is to put together your professional team. Being on your own is risky. Proverbs 15:22 warns, "Plans fail for lack of counsel, but with many advisers they succeed."

You'll want to assemble a team of experts before you find yourself backed into a corner somewhere along the way. The worst time to find help is when you are desperate. Here are some professionals who could help you:

- Insurance agent
- Accountant
- Computer expert
- Web designer
- Attorney

Set your prices according to the market.

Setting the right price for your product or service is a key element to business success. Set your prices too low and people will think you aren't a professional. Set them too high and you'll price yourself out of the market. A good place to start is to contact others in your business and determine the going range of prices. Then consider the value your product or service adds to your customer.

Higher prices are acceptable when there's a valid reason for them. If you have 25 years of experience, or you won an award for your watermelon pickles, you might justify charging higher prices. Just remember to include that information in your marketing.

Benefits of Starting a Business from Scratch

- You can live out a dream of owning your own business.
- You get to use your God-given skills and talents. When you work outside the home, you don't always use your gifts. By starting your own business, you can create the perfect job.
- Depending on the business, you set your own schedule.
- You have control over all the decisions.

Drawbacks of Starting a Business from Scratch

- It can absorb all of your time because there is always something more you could be doing.
- There's no established system of training or support.
- It's a hard road for an inexperienced entrepreneur.
- Financing could be a challenge.
- It's hard to create boundaries.
- Vacation time is hard to manage.
- You'll have to wear all the business "hats" in the beginning, which means you'll need to learn more than just the core of the business.
- Potentially longer time before realizing a profit, due to start-up expenses.

Investing in an Established Direct-Sales/Network-Marketing Business

Direct-sales companies make a huge impact on American life. A study conducted by Ernst & Young and released in February 2006 by the Direct Selling Association reported that "the direct selling industry contributed $72 billion to the U.S. economy in 2004. The $72 billion includes direct, indirect and induced impacts from $27.8 billion in wages, commissions, bonuses, and other compensation earned by the more than 13.6 million Americans who work in the direct selling industry, as well as impact from sales to customers, production activities, capital investments and tax revenue."

Chances are you know someone who loves her direct-sales business. You've probably been to a party, looked at a catalog, or had a friend go on about how her product has changed her life. When I was growing up, Tupperware parties were the rage. I bought my first bud vase as a high schooler at a Princess House party. And I've lost count of my friends who've sold Avon or Mary Kay at one time or another.

Direct-sales companies can offer wonderful ways to make income at home, whether it's pocket money or a full-time income, depending on how much time you want to invest.

By definition, a direct-sales business is one in which a product or service is sold from one individual to another, and the seller is paid a commission based on her personal sales. Think of the old-time Fuller Brush salesman who went door-to-door.

Today, most direct-sales companies are also network-marketing companies. This means that a salesperson recruits a network of other salespeople (called a downline) and receives a percentage of their sales in addition to her own. This sponsor tree can continue with an unlimited potential for residual income.

It's important to differentiate between legal network-marketing companies and illegal ones. In a legitimate company, commissions are earned only on sales to the end-user. When participants make money solely by recruiting new participants into the program and receiving a sign-up fee, that's called pyramid scheme and it's illegal. If you are investigating a company unknown to you, analyze the compensation plan to make sure you are being paid from actual sales.

Just because your neighbor is driving her second pink car and loves her experience with Mary Kay, doesn't mean it's a right fit for you. Take your time and prayerfully and practically consider your options. There are many!

If you are a very organized person, you might consider creating a graph to track some of the detailed questions, like investment costs, so you can compare apples with apples.

Ask the right questions.

- Do you love the product? If not, you won't be very convincing.
- How long has the company been around? Look for at least three years.
- What is the base commission? Rule of thumb, be suspicious of anything over 60 percent. It could mean the products are overpriced.
- What is the bonus or compensation plan? How much and when do you get paid?
- Quotas: What do you need to sell to maintain your position?
- What happens when you miss your quota?
- How much inventory do you have to maintain?
- Can you return product you don't sell if you change your mind?
- How caring are the people you'll work with? Pressure now means pressure in the future.
- What kind of training and support is offered? Is the training free or is there a charge?
- Is there a cost for training literature and programs, audiotapes and videotapes, conventions, newsletters, online access, and Web pages?
- What's their sales strategy? Does it include home sales, and catalogs? Is there an ecommerce option?
- Are they a member of the Direct Selling Association (www.dsa.org)? This is a major industry organization which monitors activities worldwide. To be a member a company needs to fulfill a one-year application process and abide by a code of ethics.

Protect yourself from fraud.

There's a general rule of thumb regarding fraud in every area of life—if it sounds too good to be true, it is. As you do your research, look for outrageous claims like the ones I found: "Retire in 90 days"; "$10,717 in less than a week"; or "No selling involved."

In our lucid moments, we know those claims aren't true. But, as King Solomon knew, there's a hunger inside many of us for a quick path to success. In Proverbs 28:19–20 he wisely reminds us, "He who works his land will have abundant food, but the one who chases fantasies will have his fill of poverty. A faithful man will be richly blessed, but one eager to get rich will not go unpunished."

The wisest piece of advice we can accept is to make sure we see "fruit" before we buy the tree. Talk to people who are selling the product and to people who have purchased the product. If you are the first one in your area to represent this company, then go to another state as part of your research. It's that important.

Finally, doubt anything that comes unsolicited whether in email or postal mail. Scoundrels know there is a longing in many hearts to be at home, and many use an aggressive approach to take advantage of people. A legitimate company attracts more representatives because of the quality of its product and customer support than through its advertising.

Benefits of Investing in a Direct-Sales Business

- There's a lower initial financial investment than most start-up businesses. Prices range between $100 and $300 for most common programs.
- Because the companies are often well known, there's already a customer base.
- The company has established marketing and training programs.
- There is already an existing product delivery system.
- The support of other salespeople can be helpful.
- There are often external rewards such as bonuses, cars, and annual conventions.
- They are great transition businesses. Most are easy to do while still working outside the home. There are possible ecommerce options. Customers go to your Web site, which features all the products.

Drawbacks of Investing in a Direct-Sales Business

- There's little personal creativity involved because everything is done for you.
- It involves direct selling.
- There are likely monthly minimum sales quotas.
- Your hours will tend to be nights and weekends.

Web Site Resources

- Direct Selling Association Web site (www.dsa.org). This is a fantastic resource. Check their member directory for lists of approved companies and links for more information.
- Internet Based Mom's Web site (www.internetbasedmoms .com). Check directory listings for Direct Sales Center. They do not endorse or research the companies, but they offer an interesting grid with information about each company listed. The site contains lots of ads, so you'll need to search through them to get to the meat.

Purchasing a Home-Based Business Franchise

Buying a home-based business franchise is an intriguing option for some. It combines some of the benefits of starting your own business with the built-in structure and support of an existing direct-sales business.

Franchises like Subway, Quiznos, and Curves top the list of Entrepreneur's strongest franchise investments in 2006. We see these types of franchises on every corner. Home-based franchises, on the other hand, aren't as obvious, but are growing in popularity. Some examples of home-based franchises include Jani-King, Geeks On Call America, Jazzercise Inc., and Chem-Dry Carpet Drapery & Upholstery Cleaning.

According to the Small Business Administration, a franchise is defined as "a legal and commercial relationship between the owner of a trademark, service mark, trade name, or advertising symbol and an individual or group wishing to use that identification in a business."

Buying a franchise is an ongoing contractual arrangement. You don't buy a Subway and then sell pizza. Customers in San

Diego and Boston count on the service and the product being the same every time they visit a Subway. The franchise owner signs a franchise agreement of typically ten years' duration to assure his or her compliance. This agreement is renewable, but is also revocable by the franchisor should it be broken. Upon renewal, there is likely a reduced fee required.

Investing in a franchise business isn't cheap. In purchasing this kind of business, the buyer invests a one-time franchise fee ranging anywhere from $5,000 to $30,000 and many are higher. There are additional operating expenses, such as equipment if necessary. Then, the owner pays an ongoing royalty fee, typically from 4 percent to 10 percent and possibly an advertising fee of 2 percent to 4 percent.

Before making a final decision, a franchisor is required to provide you with a full disclosure of all the information you'll need to make a good decision. This document is called the Uniform Franchise Offering Circular and is required by the Federal Trade Commission (FTC). Due to the complexity of this type of home-based business, it is strongly recommended by franchise experts that you consult a franchise attorney and an accountant with franchise experience before making your final decision.

Do your research to find the franchise that is right for you.

Probably the most risky part of identifying franchises is wading through the confusing waters of "business opportunities."

To find out about legitimate franchise opportunities, start with an organization you know and trust. Contact your local chamber of commerce or the Small Business Administration (SBA). Legitimate Web sites exist with lists of home-based franchise information. Entrepreneur's Web site offers one at www.entrepreneur.com. You might consider attending a trade show. One national organization that hosts business trade shows is the National Franchise and Business Opportunities Show. Their Web site includes dates around the United States (www. franchiseshowinfo.com).

Once you've identified a potential franchise, the FTC

recommends talking in person with at least ten different owners of that particular franchise before deciding. Even with organizations like the Better Business Bureau and the FTC handling complaints about scam artists, they still flourish by changing their names and flying under the radar screen. The names of ten owners should be provided you by the franchisor.

For more general information about franchises, visit the Web sites of the Small Business Administration (www.sba.gov) and the Federal Trade Commission (www.ftc.gov). There is also a national trade association of franchisees called the American Franchisee Association (www.franchisee.org). A partner of the SBA is the Small Business Development Center National Information Clearinghouse. It offers support for small business owners, including references for other franchise Web sites (http://sbdcnet.org).

Benefits of Owning a Franchise

- A home-based franchise is a "turnkey" business, offering everything you need to get started.
- You are buying a proven business model.
- You have ongoing support and training.
- Your supply issues are solved.
- You receive national advertising.

Drawbacks of Owning a Franchise

- Business operations are strictly controlled by the franchisor.
- These limits may be confining to the creative entrepreneur type.
- You may need to meet sales quotas.
- There's a high initial investment of money.

The maze of home-based business options can be confusing. I hope this chapter has clarified some of that. Before starting any business, you will be wise to get professional advice. May the Lord direct your path on this exciting journey to working at home.

CHAPTER 10

• • • • • • • •

BUSINESS 101

My son Dylan was born with an entrepreneurial spirit. From an early age, he figured out how to expand his holdings by negotiating his brothers out of their allowances. It normally involved some type of plan whereby they would pool their money to buy something big that he wanted. It usually started great, and Josh and Robbie were convinced they wanted the same item Dylan wanted. However, neither had the patience to wait, nor were they willing to sacrifice their allowances in the meantime, which they spent on Icees and other treats. So, they abandoned the savings plan every time, much to Dylan's dismay and frustration.

Realizing his brothers weren't going to be much help, Dylan set out on his own with an idea to sell Otter Pops after school for ten cents. For those who don't know, Otter Pops contain a sweetened liquid in a plastic sleeve, and when frozen they are a refreshing and affordable treat. Our home happens to be on a corner where lots of kids pass by on their way home from school, so the location was great.

Dylan used his allowance to buy a box of Otter Pops, we stuck them in the freezer, and one afternoon he set out a card table. Very quickly kids learned there were affordable treats to be bought at the Whitwers' and Dylan sold out of his first box of 100 Otter Pops within a week. Using the proceeds, he bought another box plus a large container of red licorice, which he sold for five cents per piece.

This continued for months, with Dylan reinvesting the profits and purchasing a greater assortment of candy to sell. Every week I would help Dylan tuck away some money for the purchase of something big. This little snack stand was very lucrative for a ten-year-old. In fact, he probably made $300 dollars in net profit.

Dylan worked hard and was proud of his success. His brothers had fun helping, too. They all enjoyed the PlayStation 2 Dylan purchased with the profits. This went on for quite a while until I received a call from the school principal. It seems he had received a call from an angry parent who was upset that her son was buying candy on his way home from school.

With numerous apologies for having to call, the principal explained that if we didn't shut down the candy stand, the mother would report us to the city. Immediately I called the city myself, because if we were doing something wrong, we certainly would stop selling candy.

Within a few minutes, I learned it wasn't legal to have customers physically purchase items from a residential location due to zoning laws. As disappointed as we all were, it was the right thing to close our little candy stand.

My children and I learned a lot from that experience, both affirming and constructive. We learned the right product, the right pricing, and the right placement are great components to a healthy business. But most importantly, we learned long-term success requires preparatory work.

Since we are committed to ethical business practices, I should have done some research before allowing my child to illegally sell candy on a consistent basis. A simple call to the city would have told us our idea wouldn't fly legally. I guess I was still operating in the "lemonade-stand" mentality.

Beyond the "Lemonade-Stand" Mentality

Is there an adult who didn't set up a lemonade stand at one point in his or her childhood? I sure did. In fact, I remember a hot summer day when a lone construction worker found his way to our little stand. After selling him several little plastic teacups full of lemonade for five cents each, I ran into the house for a "man-sized" glass, which we sold for a quarter.

While this is a typical childhood experience, it doesn't translate well into a professional business. It's easy to start a business and still have a lemonade-stand approach. People do it all the time. They've got a great idea for a product or service, and start their business without much thought to business basics. After all, how hard can it be? All it took Dylan was a card table and some candy. But look where that got us!

The biggest challenge with lemonade-stand thinking is that it's only concerned with the short term. There may be a burst of success, but without a solid foundation, it's likely your business will suffer over time. You may discover, like we did, that you can't legally do what you have been doing. Then you'll be faced with making very difficult and costly decisions to stay in business or go out of business, after investing a significant amount of time and effort.

One key to long-term business success is knowledge. This need for knowledge starts with the seed of an idea, continues through the start-up phase, and is critical to the ongoing management of your business.

My brother-in-law, David Gray, had a goal to run a business and started a commercial laundry business. At first, he purchased a self-service laundry in a strip mall. This allowed for walk-in traffic to provide income while he pursued commercial customers such as doctors' and dentists' offices. Over a period of years, he developed the commercial side of the business and was able to close the self-service laundry and do the work from home.

Thankfully he did his research before closing the self-service laundry. David learned the city he lived in required that he install completely new gas, electric, and water lines to run a commercial laundry service from home. Additionally, he couldn't run it from his garage as planned. He would have to build an adjacent building in the backyard. His research also showed that the adjacent city allowed him to use the existing lines and run it from his garage. Faced with this knowledge and with a desire to relocate in the near future, my sister and brother-in-law made a strategic decision to move. That was four years ago and David's business has grown steadily. He's now able to employ several other people as well.

Use available support services to help you get started.

Honestly, there's a little part of me that doesn't want to open doors that might make my life more complicated. When we started researching our businesses, we were faced with new and often complex requirements. It was like walking down a seemingly endless hallway: tax doors, licensing doors, insurance doors, legal doors, trademark doors, domain name doors, and on it went. It appeared overwhelming. I wanted to run back to our simple lemonade stand.

Business is complicated—but not impossible—to understand. I encourage you to become a learner, by tackling one subject at a time. The better educated you are, the better your chances of success in whatever work or business you choose. Some components of business we've learned on our own, and for others we've looked to experts.

The very good news is it's likely your community has free support services for you as a business owner. Every government agency wants you to succeed. Small businesses are critical to the health of a community, and free information abounds. Here are some places to check for the technical pieces of the business puzzle:

- Small Business Administration
- State department of commerce
- Local chamber of commerce
- Internal Revenue Service
- City government
- State government
- Local library
- Your bank

If all else fails, use an Internet search engine and type in "Starting a business in (your city and state)."

Think like a Christian businessperson.

A concern for Christians is being absolutely ethical in all our business dealings. While some may cut corners, we are called to a life of purity. When Jesus said, "Give to Caesar what is Caesar's," those words apply to more than money. We are to respect and work within the laws of our cities, counties, and nation. Ignorance of those laws is not a justification for breaking them. It is incumbent upon us to do the research before we start down a wrong path.

There are many ethical business owners who haven't committed their lives to following Jesus. However, there are also many unethical business owners. Consider finding or creating a network of Christian business owners who can help you stay accountable and walk you through some of your questions.

Also, it's good to consider the commandment in 2 Corinthians 6:14: "Do not be yoked together with unbelievers. For what do righteousness and wickedness have in common? Or what fellowship can light have with darkness?" Choose carefully your business partners, whether they are formal partners or people with whom you frequently do business. Each of us should determine in our own hearts what being yoked with unbelievers looks like, and avoid this situation.

Business Basics

While every business will have different requirements, there are some common components to consider. This groundwork is critical for your business efforts to have long-standing health and stability. This next section considers some issues you may need to address.

Write a business plan.

Almost every new business guide recommends starting with a business plan. I've heard it said that if you can't write a business plan, then you'll probably have trouble running your business.

A business plan is a tool to help you think through many of the details of starting your business. It can help you anticipate and solve problems, as well as set goals. *The Business Journal of Phoenix* calls it "your 'road map' toward a successful venture."

There are no strict guidelines for how a business plan looks. If it's for your use only, you can be less formal. However, if you plan to use it for financing, you'll need much more detail.

Many Web sites offer free business plan templates and sample plans. One of the best is the Small Business Administration site (www.sba.gov).

Here a few common business plan topics:
1. A full description of the business
   What's my mission statement?
   What does my business do?
   What makes it unique?
2. Marketing plan
   Can I create a demand for my business?
   Can I make any strategic alliances?
3. Competition
   What/who is my competition?
   Do they have any service gaps?
   What is my business's advantage over existing firms?
   Can I deliver a more desirable service?
4. Operating procedures
   Who will run the business and how will they do it?
   What's the management structure going to be?
   What are the qualifications of those in management?
5. Financial plan
   How much money do I need?
   What is the source of my start-up capital?
6. Financial statements
   Personal financial statements
   Pro forma income statement
   Pro forma balance sheet

Determine how you want to structure your business.

How will you run your business? This is a basic decision every home-worker needs to decide. If you are a teleworker, you will either be an employee of the firm or an independent contractor. Since you won't actually be running a business, you don't need to consider these requirements.

However, for any home-based businesses, deciding the appropriate business structure is one of the first steps and requires professional legal and tax advice. A professional will best know the requirements of your state and can accurately assess your risk and specific tax situation. As much as I wish we could operate on a handshake basis, that's just not always feasible. Every business operator should be familiar with how things work.

Most states offer support for small businesses. Great places to look for specific information are your state's department of commerce, your city's chamber of commerce, and the Small Business Administration. Check with your local library to see what small business support it may offer.

As a basic overview, here are some of the most common types of business structures and a short description of each.

1. Sole Proprietorship. This is the simplest and most common form of business organization. It's basically a business owned by one person. As such, the owner is responsible for all the debts of the business, and profit is taxed as personal income. The advantages include low start-up cost, minimum legal restrictions, and ease of running the business. One big disadvantage is unlimited liability. This means that should someone decide to sue you over a business issue, you would be personally responsible. Another concern might be fewer opportunities for financing.

2. General Partnership. This is a partnership of two or more people. A general partnership is similar to a sole proprietorship in ease of formation, debt responsibility, and simplicity of management. It also has the disadvantage of unlimited liability, and the possible challenge of decision making. It is advisable to have partnership agreements

drawn up by an attorney to outline each partner's share of income and responsibilities. The agreement should clearly outline what should happen in case the partnership is dissolved or one of the partners dies.

3. Limited Partnership. This structure is similar to the general partnership in most ways. It is a partnership of two or more people. A difference lies in the fact that of those people, at least one is identified as a general partner and is responsible for the operation and liability of the organization.

4. Limited Liability Company (LLC). This structure offers many benefits of a corporation and yet has elements of simplicity for a small business owner. It combines the limited personal liability feature of a corporation with the single taxation benefits of a sole proprietor or partnership. There is also comparative ease in operating guidelines. A distinct benefit is the protection of the owner's personal assets—or the "corporate veil." While it's more costly than a sole proprietor or partnership at the start-up, this type of business structure offers greater personal protection down the road.

5. Corporation. Two types of corporations exist: C Corporation and S Corporation.

   - C Corporation: The C Corporation is formed by law and is a completely separate business entity. As such, it is more complex and costly to initiate and maintain. A benefit of a C Corporation is that there are greater opportunities for raising capital, as potential shareholders offer money in exchange for capital stock. All stockholders have limited liability. Another benefit is the transfer of ownership by stock sale. With all good things, there is a cost. One cost of a C Corporation is that it is subject to corporate taxes and then its stockholders pay taxes on income from the corporation.

   - S Corporation: The major difference between a C Corporation and an S Corporation involves taxation. Shareholders of an S Corporation elect not to be subject to federal corporation income tax, and include all income, deduction, losses, and credits on their personal income tax.

Because my husband and I operate three different ventures from our home, we decided we needed to protect our assets. A business lawyer guided us through the decision making, and we chose a limited liability company. An additional consideration for us is that we run two distinct businesses under our LLC—an online retailer and a consulting company. For ease of recordkeeping, our lawyer recommended we also set up two "DBAs"—in other words, "Doing Business As." This allowed us to get separate bank accounts, which eases the challenges of the accounting side of the businesses.

Choose an appropriate and descriptive name for your business.

Choosing a business name is one of the most important early decisions you'll make. Your business name is your first marketing tool and your first impression. It can also be your first lawsuit if you aren't careful. A Starbucks' brainstorming session might result in the creation of a fabulous name for your business, but if Mary Smith thought of it before you, and registered it with the secretary of state, it's not available.

Before you decide on a business name, do your research. The burden is on you to assure no one has a confusingly similar name. The Small Business Association recommends checking: "lists of business names available in telephone books, libraries, city and town halls, and trade journals. Names of corporations can also be checked at the corporate division of the office of the secretary of state."

You can run free checks with the secretary of state's office and then the Internet. Even if you don't plan to open a Web site, it's a good practice to purchase the domain site just in case.

Before we started our online business, I wanted to call it Lavender Cottage. When that wasn't an available domain name, I tried Blackberry Cottage. But it was taken too. On and on it went. I tried one name after another, and all my favorites were taken. Rose Lane was the name of a park near my childhood home, and many happy hours were spent swimming and swinging on its playground. When www.roselanecottage.com was available, I snatched it up.

The next step was to register our business name with the secretary of state and the Arizona Corporation Commission. We actually had to register three names: the name of our LLC (Allwyn Priorities, LLC); my husband's consulting company (Allwyn Environmental), and our online retailer (Rose Lane Cottage).

Another way to protect your business name is to trademark it. In his book *The Complete Work-at-Home Companion,* Herman Holtz offers this concise definition of a trademark: "A trademark is some distinctive name, slogan, logo, design or other mark that someone uses to identify and distinguish his or her company, goods or service."

Although you aren't required to trademark your business name, if your company goals are to expand into other states, you are wise to do so. This would apply to anyone who runs a Web site or mail order business. Registering a trademark is done through the US Patent and Trademark Office and costs approximately $325. For more information, visit the Web site at www.uspto.gov.

Please check with your individual state regarding specific requirements for registering a business name.

Here are some general tips for choosing a business name:

- Research shows that names telling something about the product are more successful than those that are vague.
- Think about names evoking feelings you want customers to experience: satisfied, contented, energized.
- Find words relating to your service or product, such as colors, gemstones, animals, or plants. When my nephew opened a tactical supply company he chose the diamondback rattler as his theme. Now, Diamondback Tactical is growing and selling supplies to those men and women who protect our country. Who wouldn't want to be as swift and powerful as the diamondback rattler?
- Avoid generic names like Tom's Cleaning. They are hard to remember and more difficult to trademark.
- Avoid location names. That limits your further growth. An excellent example is Kentucky Fried Chicken, which now

calls itself KFC. A dual benefit of the name change was removing the geographic location and allowing consumers to forget how the chicken is actually cooked.

Develop a professional team.

Proverbs 15:22 advises us, "Plans fail for lack of counsel, but with many advisers they succeed."

No matter how small or big your business plans, you will need professional advice. My husband and I have found, without exception, that everyone is willing to help us succeed. Why? Not only are they good people, but each of them benefits when we are successful. As you start your business, consider developing relationships with the following groups of people:

- Banker. There are still bank managers who want to know your name. They can help you with questions or resolve problems. Additionally, should you ever apply for a loan, having a personal relationship with a banker is a good foundation.
- Accountant. Our accountant has provided a wealth of information. He helped us set up our accounting system, was patient as we asked hundreds of questions, and because his office is in our hometown, he's knowledgeable about legal requirements for business.
- Graphic designer. We work with a wonderful Christian woman who does professional graphic design work from home while caring for her two daughters. For a fair price she designed a logo, letterhead, and business cards for us. Nothing can replace a professional appearance.
- Lawyer. Finding a good business lawyer was one of our best investments. While it's possible to do a lot of the legal paperwork yourself, because our business is our sole source of income, we couldn't make a mistake. It was worth every penny.
- Insurance agent. You should check with your insurance agent about your homeowners insurance and running a business from home. Ask if your auto insurance might be reduced now that you aren't commuting. Since my husband

and I are both self-employed, our insurance agent found the best health and dental insurance plan for us. Also, consider whether professional liability insurance is needed.

Meet all the legal requirements for operating a business.

A home-based business is subject to the same licensing and permit laws as any other business. This means you'll need to learn the different requirements that all levels of government require. In addition, if your neighborhood has a homeowners association, research any restrictions. These are legally binding.

For example, the US government requires you to have an employer identification number. If you are buying wholesale and reselling a product, you'll need a resale number to pay the sales taxes. Your city will require a business license. My city also has special regulatory licenses. For instance, if you are growing and selling herbs, they want to know.

Although the Internet has lots of detailed information, nothing can replace a face-to-face appointment with a knowledgeable city or state employee.

Starting a business is a little like buying your first house. It involves a brand-new vocabulary, the help of a variety of experts, a lot of patience, and hard work. There's still a lot of maintenance once you move in, but it gets easier each month.

If you have never dealt with the details of running a business, prepare to have new questions every month. A great resource to walk you through many of your questions is the organization SCORE—Counselors to America's Small Business. SCORE is a nonprofit organization with more than 10,500 volunteers who are either working or retired business owners, executives, and corporate leaders. The organization is committed to the success of small businesses. They offer online advice, one-on-one local business counseling, workshops, and many how-to articles and templates on their Web site www.score.org.

Commit your plans to the Lord.

Proverbs 16:3 says, "Commit to the Lord whatever you do, and your plans will succeed."

We can strive to succeed, but without God's help, all our human efforts will be like chaff blown away by the wind. The children's song reminds us that a wise man builds his house upon the rock. The foundation of our business must be our personal commitment to the Lord and an understanding that He holds our success in His hands.

We must always keep in mind that the credit for our success doesn't go to good planning (although that helps), to wise financial decisions (although that's a must), to our intelligence, or to the strength of our arms. The Scriptures remind us in Proverbs 16:9 that "in his heart a man plans his course, but the LORD determines his steps."

What a different approach to business! Although we have human experts around us, we can approach the Creator of knowledge and the Giver of wisdom for advice and direction. Now that's the best Business 101 advice I've ever heard.

CHAPTER 11
• • • • • • • •

FINANCING THE BUSINESS

Financing a large venture should be a very prayerful decision for a Christian. As discussed in early chapters, we are like servants entrusted with our Master's resources. He is always watching to see how we manage our time, personal talents, and, of course, money.

The parable of the talents, found in Matthew 25, demonstrates the importance of the servant (us) investing the resources given to him (us again), to produce an increase for his Master. Notice I said for "his Master" and not for him. This paradigm shift in our heart attitude is important. It's not about us! The story illustrates that God is pleased with our efforts when we yield a return on our investment for Him.

Because financing a business often involves borrowing, we need to weigh every choice against the truth of the Scriptures. Additionally, this is an area where we need wise advice from mature, biblically based, and financially wise counselors.

If you have financial counselors at your local church, ask for one-on-one advice. If you don't have local resources, then one of the best known and most respected organizations in Christian circles is Crown Financial Ministries (www.crown.org). Crown states its mission this way: "Equipping people worldwide to learn, apply, and teach God's financial principles so they may know Christ more intimately, be free to serve Him, and help fund the Great Commission."

This ministry's Web site is filled with biblical advice on every aspect of money. I encourage you to visit it often when you have questions.

Before getting into specifics on how to raise capital for your business, let's consider what the Scriptures have to say about borrowing. While it isn't specifically prohibited in the Scriptures, it isn't encouraged. In fact, every biblical reference discourages borrowing. Here are two examples:

"The rich rule over the poor, and the borrower is servant to the lender" (Proverbs 22:7).

"For the Lord your God will bless you as he has promised, and you will lend to many nations but will borrow from none. You will rule over many nations but none will rule over you" (Deuteronomy 15:6).

When we do borrow, we are to repay:

"If a man borrows an animal from his neighbor and it is injured or dies while the owner is not present, he must make restitution" (Exodus 22:14).

"The wicked borrow and do not repay, but the righteous give generously" (Psalm 37:21).

Borrowing is not God's best for His people. As the Scriptures state, borrowing makes us a servant to the lender. We are to serve one Master and that's God. Very simply stated, the best way to fund your business is to do it with your own savings. With this approach, you may need to start your business slowly or on a smaller scale.

Don't get trapped into thinking bigger is better.

Len and Deborah Ehrfurth are very wise financial counselors and successful home-based business entrepreneurs. Len advises business owners to start small:

Start with little to no debt, keeping your overhead as low as possible. The pressure to produce a large income from the beginning to cover expenses is too demanding and stressful. As the business and income grow put a portion, 20-25%, into needed equipment and supplies. Continue to do so until the business is the size you desire. Then invest the extra for yourselves while maintaining the business level required for proper operation.

Don't get trapped into thinking you must start off "big." Statistically, 50% of all businesses fail in the first year and the failure rate grows to 80% by the second year. High debt and overhead are two of the leading causes of failures. Work hard to build a business with as little debt as you can and you will make it well past the failure rate and allow yourself to not become another statistic.

Len and Deborah are proof this philosophy works as they've lived it for more than 20 years. Len runs several businesses from home, and has never been in debt, not even for their home. Their careful spending and sharp business skills allowed Deborah to always stay home and raise their three children, serve in ministry, and even write a book of devotions on money and finances called *Meditations on Money* (www.MeditationsOnMoney.com).

Follow scriptural principles about borrowing money.

If borrowing is part of your plan, then it's best to follow biblical guidelines. Crown Financial Ministries offers this advice, "There are three fundamental scriptural principles related to business borrowing: borrowing should only be occasional, avoid signing surety on a loan, and stay out of long-term debt." (Used by permission of Crown Financial Ministries.)

In essence, we should not make borrowing a habit, never cosign on a loan for someone else or borrow without a way to repay, and pay off our debts as quickly as possible.

Before we address options for raising business capital, I want to strongly advise you to get a professional opinion before making a decision on how to fund your business. This advice could come from a financial expert, accountant, or lawyer. The information in this chapter is not meant to be professional counsel, simply an overview of options available.

Raising Capital for Your Business

As you consider how to raise money for your start-up business, you may need to use a variety of sources. First pool your available personal resources, making sure you have enough in savings to pay your bills for at least three months. Then as you consider other options, do not put your financial security at risk by placing all your eggs in one basket. If you do need to borrow money, do it wisely and for the smallest amount necessary.

Sell your assets.

This is at the top of the list because it doesn't involve borrowing. If you are following your dream, then selling some of your possessions should be a minor sacrifice to achieve it. Consider selling recreational items first such as pool tables, boats, time-shares, and second properties. You might have jewelry, rugs, or furniture that would bring in some cash. Also, consider downsizing your home or getting a more affordable car.

Leverage the value of your home.

If your home has appreciated in value, you might qualify for a home equity loan. Banks are more comfortable loaning against your home because they know in the worst-case scenario you can sell it to repay the loan. If you go this direction, only borrow a portion of what's available to you—perhaps 25–30 percent. You can also set aside some of the money to repay the loan until your business is self-supporting. You might also consider refinancing your home to reduce your monthly payments.

Borrow against your investments.

It's possible to take out a loan from some 401(k)s, IRAs, and life insurance plans. Be prepared to meet their stringent requirements for paying the loan back, or you'll find yourself socked with high interest rates and early withdrawal penalties.

Consider carefully whether to borrow from family or friends.

Borrowing from family or friends is a little like scuba diving in uncharted waters. You can find beautiful tropical fish or man-eating sharks. Because borrowing money can separate even the closest of friends, this idea comes packed with warnings.

1. Present them with copies of your business plan and ask them to pray over the decision.
2. Put everything in writing. Don't assume you or your lender will remember the details. A written agreement will diffuse disagreements.
3. Follow professional standards. If you don't approach this loan transaction from a professional standpoint, your laxity may backfire down the line. If the day ever comes when you approach a bank or investors for capital, they will review your history with a fine-tooth comb. Any errors or inconsistencies could delay or cost you an opportunity. Consider having a lawyer oversee the process.
4. Clarify that a loan isn't a partnership. If you borrow $5,000 from Uncle Joe, he may think he's got a say in how you do business. Keep the business agreement separate from your relationship.
5. Pay the loan back promptly. Consider paying in quarterly increments in case one month you're low on cash.

Take out a bank loan.

Before applying for a bank loan, you'll need to make sure your credit history is solid. Get a copy of your credit report and take action to clean up anything that looks spotty. Once a year you can get a copy of your credit report for free on Annualcreditreport .com. It's very important to close credit accounts you no longer use. Make a phone call to close the account, and ask that written verification be sent to you and the credit agency reporting the open account. Open accounts show a lender that you have the potential to rack up your debt, thereby making you a greater risk.

You need to be completely professional and prepared with a thoroughly researched and well-documented business plan. This plan will demonstrate your ability to manage the business and explain your plan for paying back the loan.

The purpose for which the funds are to be used is a very important factor in deciding what kind of loan to request. There are two basic types of loans: lines of credit and installment loans. A line of credit offers the borrower funds as they are needed, up to a predetermined limit. An installment loan is an agreement to provide a lump sum amount of money at the beginning of the loan. The loan is paid back in equal amounts over the course of a number of years.

Schedule a meeting with a bank loan officer at your personal bank before initiating any loan application. This fulfills two purposes. First, you become more than an account number. Even though we live in a society where more and more business is done without human interaction, it is still a person who makes the final decision. You can convey much about your character in a face-to-face meeting. Second, you can learn about your options for loans and get tips on how to best prepare.

If your loan is denied, ask the lending officer to tell you why. Carefully consider the answer and refine your loan package accordingly. Every lender is going to assure that you and your business are worth the risk. Since they do this every day of the year, chances are they will see a weakness you might have missed. Another thing to consider is that some banks cater to small businesses. Do some research before trying again.

Check into the Small Business Administration Loan Guarantee.

Under its Basic 7(a) Loan Guaranty, the US Small Business Administration (SBA) works to help fund small businesses. To clarify, the SBA doesn't directly loan money to business owners. Instead it sets the guidelines for the loans and provides a guarantee to the lender should there be a default on the loan. The SBA's financial partners, like your local bank, actually make the loans.

The SBA works with start-up businesses and provides funds for "most sound business purposes including working capital, machinery and equipment, furniture and fixtures, land and building (including purchase, renovation and new construction), leasehold improvements, and debt refinancing (under special conditions)," according to the SBA Web site (www.sba.gov).

Before applying for an SBA guaranteed loan, you must first apply for a conventional loan and be turned down. Another plus for a new business is that lenders consider the projected income of your business, not just historical cash flow, when making a decision.

Use a limited partnership as a way to fund your business.

A limited partnership is one way to organize your business legally, but it may also be a way to fund your venture. Limited partnerships consist of a group of people who contribute capital to the company and have limited liability to the extent of their investment. There are also general partners who manage the company and have unlimited personal liability for its debts. My first job out of college was for a limited partnership of doctors. They had joined together to build and manage medical offices. I worked in the office of the general partners.

This is a very legally intense approach and one that necessitates professional counsel. Although it is a funding pathway, it also puts more pressure on you to provide ongoing feedback to your partners and a timely return on their investments.

Contact a venture capital company for funds.

Venture capital companies exist to provide equity financing to businesses. This involves selling a portion of your business to outside investors. The good news is you don't have to pay it back, but you also have investors looking over your shoulder and a portion of your business is owned by an outside interest. This is a very competitive pathway as venture capitalists review a great number of proposals, but approve few. Normally, venture capitalists are looking to invest $250,000 to $1,000,000, which is more than many home-based businesses need.

According to Brian E. Hill and Dee Power, coauthors of *Inside Secrets to Venture Capital,* you'll need a show of management strength to impress this group of investors. "Put together a strong, experienced management team, with people who have been successful in the past. The importance of a strong management team cannot be overstressed. Lack of a strong management team is the number one reason why VCs decline to invest."

Finding start-up funding is a challenge. Everyone is a beginner at some point in his or her life, and this may be the most difficult hurdle in starting your business. But don't let the challenge discourage you from pursuing your dream. Every successful business started somewhere. Be smart, be prepared, be creative, and be persistent. If at all possible, don't borrow money. That way, you can pursue your goals without the weight of debt and be on your way to a financially healthy future.

CHAPTER 12

· · · · · · · ·

GROWING YOUR BUSINESS

When I was a junior in college, I remember a sign placed strategically outside the counseling offices. Its simple message profoundly affects my approach to business today.

At this very large and busy university, it was decidedly important to complete a senior checkout. This document outlined the courses a student needed to take during his or her next two to three semesters in order to graduate. Due to its importance, the university encouraged students to complete this form and have it approved by a counselor, which was my reason for being there.

As a visual tool, someone had designed a poster around the words *Plan Ahead for Your Senior Checkout*. I wasn't impacted by the words as much as the way they were written. They started at the left of the poster in big, bold strokes, but three-quarters of the way across, the letters got smaller and smaller, and eventually curved down the right side of the poster. It was obvious the writer realized too late he hadn't planned effectively and ran out of room.

What an accurate portrayal of so many elements of life and business. Many times we begin with the best intentions and a soaring confidence level. We love what we are doing and have high hopes for our home-based work. Then along comes real life with its annoying habit of nudging us off our path with distractions or challenges. We don't experience immediate success; it's harder than we thought and we become discouraged.

One problem is that most of us operate in a reactive mode rather than proactive. In starting a business, so much of our energy is focused in the business that we neglect to focus on the business. Unless you are an overnight success, with customers knocking down your door, you'll need to focus on your business by developing a marketing plan for growth.

Although most business owners loathe marketing, it is actually one of my favorite parts of running a business. That's because my college degree and professional career were focused on promotion. With a degree in journalism with an emphasis on public relations, I love the planning and implementation of ways to increase business.

There are three truths I've learned over the years about marketing:

1. You have to plan. It's a very ineffective and wasteful use of time and money to approach marketing and growth from a haphazard perspective.
2. Your plan should include measurable goals. Where do you want to be in three months, six months, or a year? Be specific.
3. You must step out of the day-to-day routine to plan. The best planning came when we were away from our offices. These planning sessions might be held in another office, or even in another city. They were always fun and, boy, did the creativity flow.

I wish you and I could meet at a retreat center in the mountains or by the ocean to go over this material together, but since we can't, hopefully the steps outlined in this chapter will equip you to identify where you want your business to go and then help you design a plan to get there. It's essential to define your purpose for being in business, the people you hope to reach, and the means you will use to reach them.

Clarifying Your Vision

A mission statement is a foundational piece of growing a business. Sometimes called a purpose statement, it can be one sentence or a paragraph, so long as it states your goals and purpose for existing. Once complete, it can help guide your decision making. Here's one of ours:

Rose Lane Cottage offers a collection of cottage-style home and garden accessories to help women create a warm and welcoming home for their families and guests. We also seek to offer practical help for embracing home and family through a blog and enewsletter.

This mission statement reminds me that the goal of our business is more than selling products. It's helping women create a "nest" out of their home, and then making the most of what God has given them. That's much more compelling and inspiring to me than just selling lamps, clocks, and tablecloths. It also reminds me that our target market is women, which helps direct our marketing efforts.

Spend some time writing a short mission statement for your business. Keep it short and simple. Have it reflect your values.

Author David Schaefer in his book *Surefire Strategies for Growing Your Home-Based Business* calls it "refining your 'so what.'" He advises, "In ten words that a high school student would understand, answer the questions: What do I do? Who do I do it for?" Moving from there, he recommends answering these questions as well: "When people work with me, they get the following benefits"; and "I make my client's life or business new, different or better because . . ."

Armed with the answers to these questions, you are better prepared to move ahead and make plans for the success and growth of your business.

Identifying Your Target Market

One of the most helpful concepts in marketing is understanding your target market. Who is going to buy this product or service? By knowing whom you are trying to reach, you can customize your approach to reaching them.

The more specific you get, the better. Your mission statement might include a broad market like ours (women); but as you refine your marketing plans you'll want to identify specific groups of women who will benefit from what you offer. Saying that women are different from one another is an understatement. Not only are women in different life seasons (single, stay-at-home mothers, married-no children, empty nesters), but women have grown up in drastically different generations. We are reaching women who grew up in the Great Depression (like my mother) and Gen-Xers (like my nieces).

Once you have identified your target market, you can proceed with designing a multilayered, creative approach to promotion.

Writing Your Marketing Plan

There's no formal template for creating a marketing plan. You can start with a pencil and a pad of paper and a list of ways to promote your business over the next 3, 6, or 12 months.

Your marketing plan will include the different ways you will promote your business. Especially as a new business operator, you'll want to have a multilayered approach to marketing. If you put all your money into advertising in the local paper, you'll be disappointed if you find your target market gets his or her news from the radio. Until you know more about what works and what doesn't, be varied. If you know your target market intimately, then, by all means, incorporate specific ways to reach that market.

Consider including deadlines, such as personal deadlines for completing a task or deadlines for submitting ads or press releases.

As you consider what your budget allows, here are some avenues to market your business:

- Public relations
- Advertising

- Direct mail
- Networking
- Internet

Let's take a look at each of these in turn.

Take advantage of free public relations opportunities.

Public relations (PR) is a broad term, and differs from advertising in that it is free publicity. In the corporate world, the PR department might plan a special event, sponsor a fund-raiser, answer questions from the media, and send out press releases on newsworthy events and changes happening within their company. For a small business owner, one component of public relations that works well is a press release.

A press release is a way to communicate newsworthy information about your business to the media. Basically, it's a news or feature article you write and submit to the local paper, television station, or radio station. If they believe it has merit, they will include it. When they do, not only do you have free advertising, but you have the added benefit of it coming from an unbiased third party.

Here some public relations basics:

- Create a media list. You can do this by researching local magazines, newspapers, and radio and television stations that accept press releases. You'll find some of this information in phone books or on the Internet. Once you have the names and phone numbers, start making calls. Ask the following questions:
  1. Do they accept press releases?
  2. How do they like to receive them? Fax, mail, email?
  3. To whom should they be addressed?
  4. What are their deadlines?
- Pick a newsworthy topic. Once you've got your list, come up with some newsworthy information. The fact that you exist probably won't be newsworthy to most publications. What might be interesting is if you are starting to offer a new service or hosting a special event. Start reading the business section of the newspaper for ideas on what stories

they print. Another type of press release is a feature story. A feature isn't presented as "news," but as a topic of interest. When I worked in the retirement industry, one of our residents was the first woman inducted into the Women's Air Corps. She was in her 80s and had a colorful history. We contacted the local paper, who assigned a reporter to write an article about her life, of course mentioning where she lived. It was a wonderful story and we got the side benefit of being mentioned in the paper.

- Write the press release. Always write in third person. Don't say, "I'm offering a new service." Instead, write, "Family Tree-4-U is now offering . . ." If you are writing a basic news release, include the "five Ws" at the top of your story.
  1. Who: Who is doing whatever it is that is happening
  2. What: What this business is doing
  3. When: When it will happen, or when it happened
  4. Where: The specific location
  5. Why: The church is raising funds for a new food bank building

Keep your release to four or five paragraphs double-spaced. If the release flows on to a second page, make sure your contact information is on both pages. At the end of the release, put *-end-* or *-30-* centered below the final paragraph.

At the top of every press release include your name, title, phone number, email address, and the date you are sending the release. Make it as easy as possible for the reporter to contact you for more information.

There's no guarantee you'll get a press release published. But by picking a newsworthy topic and by writing your release well, you increase your chances of getting free publicity for your business.

Research, compare, and choose advertising vehicles that reach your market.

Advertising can be expensive, but if well placed, it's an effective marketing tool. Seek out smaller publications that are reaching your market. Most publications have specific demographic information available to advertisers. Before making any decisions, ask for information about rates and do a thorough comparison of your options. When you create your media call list for press releases, save yourself a second phone call by asking for an advertising packet at the same time. For advertising to be most effective, choose smaller size ads and opt for repetition. Don't forget radio advertising.

Check into personalized and targeted direct-mail campaigns.

Huge, impersonal direct-mail campaigns can be expensive and tricky. At best you'll get a 3 percent response rate to your offer. This might be a good choice somewhere down the road.

Another option for direct mail is a smaller, more personalized approach. Once you develop an existing and potential client base, you can send out mailings throughout the year. Always tie it in with some benefit to your customer. My accountant sends out a tax update newsletter in January, just when I'm starting to think about that annual responsibility. Every so often, my Mary Kay representative sends me a colorful catalog of new products that will make me look younger and prettier, or so they say.

You can create simple mailings using postcards to announce the addition of a new service or to offer a discount for a period of time. If you learn personal information about your customers, send out birthday cards or anniversary cards. Your direct mailings don't have to be four-color expensive pieces to be effective.

Use the Internet to market and advertise your business.

Without a doubt, the Internet offers the most exciting number of new options for marketing your business. No business should put all its marketing dollars into the Internet, but it is a tool to be considered in your plan. Due to its importance, chapter 13 is devoted to navigating the Internet. Here are some components to learn more about:

- Web site. You can create a simple Web site easily using one of the many programs available. A basic use of your Web site will be for potential customers to get more information about your service or product. If you want to bring in traffic to your business through your Web site, you'll need to learn about search engine optimization. Since this is a very detailed process with requirements that change monthly, I strongly advise getting professional help.

- Blog. Anyone can start a blog for free. Some writer friends maintain blogs to publish their thoughts and stories. Tod and I have a blog to offer articles on how to develop family relations, organize your home, and balance your life. We provide this as a service to our customers and anyone seeking some practical help with life. It's our obvious hope that our blog readers will also visit our site and purchase our products.

- Discussion groups. Online discussion groups are great places to network. If you set up a Web site, you can start your own discussion group with different forums or themes. At the Transition Home Web site, we have forums on budgeting, telecommuting, home-based businesses, and more. People post questions and other people provide answers based on their personal experiences. Most discussion groups allow you to put your personal Web site or blog address in your signature line, thereby leading others to learn more about you.

Use networking as a natural opportunity to share your company's mission.

Networking is a time-honored marketing tool. It just means meeting others who might need your services or product at some time. It also means meeting people you might possibly help down the road.

Janet Drez, author of *Putting the Pieces Together,* writes, "Networking is about sharing, giving and nurturing. It's about being 100% committed to the success of those around you, who will, in turn become 100% committed to your success."

When viewed from this angle, networking isn't so scary because it takes the pressure off. No longer do you need to have a polished sales pitch. You can relax and focus on others, and then naturally share what you do.

Networking avenues include chambers of commerce, trade organizations, and anywhere potential customers gather.

However, if you attend and hope others approach you, you'll be disappointed. Look for someone standing alone and introduce yourself. Ask open-ended questions and listen carefully. People are just people, longing to be known and appreciated. Your attention to their words will go much farther than your sales pitch.

Be very, very careful to not be pushy. I've been in groups where someone obviously saw me as a customer and had an agenda to promote her business. I didn't feel valued as a person, which diminished my interest in anything she had to sell.

Jesus was the perfect networker. As He met and shared the good news of the kingdom of God with people, He truly loved them and cared about their spiritual, emotional, and physical needs. Jesus saw people's eternities in the balance with every interaction, with every meal He shared, and with every conversation He had. As a result, people were drawn to Jesus and received His free gift of eternal life. As I pursue marketing my home-based business, I ask God for a heart like Jesus to see beyond the surface of those I meet. It is my ultimate dream to be used to further God's kingdom in every aspect of my life.

Additional Considerations for the Christian Home-Worker

In Ephesians 5:16, Paul admonishes us that we should be wise, "making the most of every opportunity." What sets us apart from the hordes of people who work every day, either inside the home or out, to provide for their families? The fact that our work is a calling, a higher calling in which we can model the love of Christ in our dealings with our customers.

We can look for opportunities to serve and minister to our customers.

My friend Shari Braendel is a very successful home-based entrepreneur. I first met her when she presented a seminar called "What Not to Wear." It was there I discovered my skin coloring was actually "autumn" as opposed to the "winter" I'd been told

20 years before. This meant that the royal blues and hot pinks in my wardrobe should be replaced by golds and browns. But that's another story.

What I learned from Shari was to add value to your customer's life. You see, in addition to teaching seminars, Shari is also a very successful Mary Kay Cosmetics director. But Shari's not all about making the sale. She cares how each customer feels about herself, and not just on the surface. A woman's confidence is a precarious thing, and Shari knows that the right outfit and makeup are just part of the package. Shari invests herself in others by helping women see that their true value and worth are found in Christ. I believe this is the reason Shari is also a good businesswoman.

What value can you add beyond the product or service you provide? Consider this as you seek to grow your business using traditional marketing methods.

We can work hard to really get to know and keep in contact with our customers.

My pastor, Brian Anderson, is an expert at "customer service." Although our church averages between 4,000 and 5,000 people in attendance each week, somehow Brian manages to remember most newcomers' names. This is a shocking thing to people, and I've heard it said this was one of the reasons they gave the church a second chance. Brian then continues to amaze members by remembering personal things about their lives. He's an outstanding role model for a small business owner.

In a world of impersonalization, you can set yourself apart by remembering personal details about your customers. I've learned that Brian takes the time to write down information on index cards and regularly reviews them. Every member has a photo taken and Brian reviews those as well.

To come anywhere close to this attention to detail, you need a system for remembering. This can be as simple as your own index card file, or you can invest in a computer database system.

Once you've got a system in place, use this system to follow up on leads and to check back with customers. I'm confident your personal touch will set you apart as a businessperson worth knowing; but even more than that, you can show your customers that they themselves are valued.

We can cultivate our expertise and share it with others.

If you're anything like me, you tend to consider other people as the "experts." I figure there's always someone out there with more knowledge and experience than me. Actually, that's pretty much the truth. But that doesn't mean I can't increase my knowledge and experience and share that with someone else.

God has called me at this time and place to do what I do. That means the knowledge and experience I have are valuable to Him. It also means that He sees my potential and knows better than I what my future holds. I believe God is calling me to step out in confidence and share what He has given me so far.

How does this apply to you? God has called and gifted you too. You have a combination of experiences, knowledge, training, education, and personal talent that no one else has. As you grow in your knowledge, consider how you can share it with others.

One way is to become a public speaker. There are conferences and seminars being held across the country looking for workshop leaders. Research those in your area, review the subjects covered, and identify a topic you could address. Then send a letter to the coordinator of the conference offering your services. It's possible the conference board may pay you; but even if it doesn't, you are getting your name out there as an expert in your field. I did this with a Christian women's leadership conference, and I was asked to lead a workshop. The next year I suggested two other workshops and was invited back.

Another avenue for sharing your knowledge is local and national media. As a magazine editor, I am always looking for articles by authors with a unique personal experience and expertise. If you have writing skill, consider writing a how-to article and submitting it to a national magazine. Normally you can include a bio and often an email address or Web site address. To get started, purchase a writer's market guide available through any large bookstore. These guides contain a wealth of information including submission guidelines.

In addition to national media, local newspapers and magazines often look for feature stories and experts to interview. Regional publications are often best discovered in the yellow pages. Don't forget radio stations.

A few years ago, I received a call from a local radio station asking if I would address the cover article of the most recent *Newsweek* magazine. The article talked about the great demands placed on women today. The radio team knew I was on staff with Proverbs 31 Ministries and wanted a Christian women's view of how to balance the myriad tugs on a woman's skirt. The radio interview was a great experience and I got two speaking engagements as a result.

Although I wish I'd initiated that call, it gave me a great idea for marketing. Keep your eyes open for current events and trends that relate to your field of expertise. When you find one you are qualified to address, make a call or send an email to the assignment desk at your local media.

Marketing isn't just for the experts. Every businessperson can learn some marketing tools and apply them with success. To be most effective, marketing involves making a plan that includes a variety of methods. I believe the most productive efforts are those that take a service approach rather than a cold-sales approach. Consider what service you can provide others and allow your marketing program to develop from there.

CHAPTER 13

• • • • • • • •

INTERNET BASICS

A s a B.C. ("Before Computers") child, I must admit that the Internet alternately scares and intrigues me. It enters our home with dangers I can't always anticipate, I have trouble sifting through all the information available, and the technology overwhelms me. With all the worry it causes, I often wonder—is it worth the trouble?

And yet, when my son wants to research ancient Roman history and confirm the historical accuracy of gladiator weapons used in the movie *Spartacus,* I'm very thankful for the Internet. When I write a devotion that encourages a mom in South Africa, I'm grateful for this invention. When my husband and I receive an order for our online business, which helps support our family, I wonder—how can we live without this thing?

For those of us who still don't fully get this computer stuff, a few definitions and a touch of history might be helpful. The Internet as we know it started in 1969 with four interconnected computers. In most simplistic terms, it is now a global network connecting millions of computers, in which any computer can communicate with another computer. The World Wide Web (Web) is a subset of the Internet and is how we access information, such as on a Web site. Another subset of the Internet familiar to most of us is email.

Whatever my personal opinion of the Internet happens to be at the moment, it is an invaluable tool for the home-based worker. However, I have learned that the concept of "build it and they will come" doesn't apply in the world of cyberspace. If you create a Web site and then sit back waiting for customers to flock to you, you'll be greatly disappointed. Because it takes creativity and work, in this chapter we will review some of the opportunities for expanding your knowledge and expanding your business through the Internet. Mind you, this is only an overview. My hope is you'll get your interest sparked and give you a baseline from which to continue with your own research.

Web Sites

With over 80 million sites accessible on the Web, a person can learn everything from how to fold napkins to how to run a multimillion dollar corporation. Web sites serve many functions and are used to advertise and sell products and services, share and solicit information, and promote ideas to name a few. For today's business owner, a Web site is as much a necessity as a business card and logo. It's probably unrealistic, but I expect every professional business to have a Web site and am immediately suspicious when they don't.

Just as you would never go to an important meeting in shorts and a T-shirt, your Web site should be produced and maintained in a professional and relevant manner. It speaks volumes about your professionalism and attention to detail. In the world of Web sites, content is king. Yours should constantly be reinvented with fresh, interesting, and informative copy. There's nothing more discouraging than visiting a Web site only to see a note saying, "Last updated five years ago."

Choose a domain name.

The first step to developing your Web site is choosing and then registering a domain name. In chapter 10, I offered some suggestions for your business name, which is often used as a domain name. If not using a business name, keep your domain name descriptive and short, and choose the proper extension. Focus on the Family's Web site is a good example: family.org. "Family" sums up their target market and their ministry and "org" indicates nonprofit. The Internet Corporation for Assigned Names and Numbers (ICANN) is responsible for managing and coordinating the domain name system and features a list of available extensions and accredited domain registrars on their Web site (www.icann.org/registrars/accredited-list.html).

Find a host.

The next step is to find a good Web host. Expect to pay about $10 to $20 per month to maintain a basic Web site, and more if you'll need extensive pages or will sell products. Some Web hosts will do domain search and registration for you as part of their package. To research potential Web hosts, ask others you know who currently maintain a Web site. They could be your church, a local business, or even someone you don't know. If you find a Web site you like, email the owner and ask who they use. Most people are happy to share their experiences, both good and negative.

As you compare your options, consider these elements:
- Price
- Amount of storage space
- Number of email addresses included
- Is Web page software included?
- What are the file transfer limitations? (How much "stuff"— logos/graphics/copy—can you put on your site?)
- Are there options for a shopping cart and secure ecommerce?
- Is automatic data backup included?
- Can you get site statistics? (Can you track how many people have visited your site?)
- What kind of setup and customer service support is available?

- Are multimedia/CGI scripts included? (Do you ever want to include sound or video, or use information gathered on your site in marketing?)

Create your site.

You can set up a Web site in a day for less than $100 or you can take months and spend over $10,000. There really are a multitude of options for today's businessperson. How you actually create your Web site will come down to how much time and money you can invest in this component of your business. Because of its importance, I encourage you to make it a priority. Even though you can slap one together in an afternoon, don't.

An affordable and easy way to create a site is by using a template. You'll have some color and design options, but it's basically a fill-in-the-blank approach. These templates are readily available through most Web hosts. If you've got all your information written, and design elements (such as photos) ready, you can get this up and running quickly. One advantage to a template is the ease of making changes down the road. A drawback is you end up with a cookie-cutter look with very little customization available—unless you can write code.

There are some complete packages available for those who want to operate an online store. Some providers include Amazon .com zStores, Yahoo!Store, and GoECart. The provider can pull all the ingredients together to get you up and selling relatively quickly.

A notch up in complexity, but still doable, is to purchase Web page editor software. This can be purchased at a computer supply store from $50 to $500. Some examples include Macromedia Dreamweaver and Microsoft FrontPage. This method provides flexibility, creativity, and customization. While you won't need much programming knowledge, prepare to spend time learning. Of course, once you've become an "expert," you can do much more with your site.

The highest level of difficulty in creating a Web site is to design it from scratch. This will require you to either have or to acquire extensive programming knowledge. Your time investment to create the site will greatly increase, but you will save money and expand your creative options by doing it yourself. If you go this route, consider some type of professional training or education. A community college or technical school might be options. Online training options also exist. One programming site is W3 Schools (www.w3schools.com).

The alternative to doing it yourself is to hire a professional Web designer. Although it will cost you more upfront and as you pay for future revisions, you will end up with a more professional and search engine–friendly site.

Organize your Web site in a way that drawsand keeps people's interest.

Regardless of how you create your Web site, it should be organized around some common guidelines. Statistics show that a potential customer will decide in seconds whether to stay on a site. Since the home page is a visitor's first impression, make sure it clearly conveys your company image, mission, products, and services. It should be informative, yet attractive and interesting. Most people visiting your site will want to see at a glance what they can expect to find on your back pages. Use words that are commonly known so your guest can navigate around your site with ease.

When I visit a Web site, I'm looking for information. Nothing annoys me more than clicking on what looks like a link to information, only to discover one ad after another for a book that will give me information I want. While you don't want to give away all your knowledge, offer something worthwhile and informative to your site visitor. After all, why would someone hire you or buy your product if they don't have confidence in your knowledge? And how can they have confidence in your knowledge if you don't share some of it with them? To encourage return visitors, offer a variety of information and change your content frequently.

Spend money, time, and effort making your Web site look professional. A graphic designer can help add design elements you wouldn't have considered. Check and double-check your spelling, grammar, and punctuation. Avoid slang and any comment that could be interpreted as inappropriate. If you are selling a product or service, provide a detailed description of what the buyer will receive. Before going live with your site, ask others to review every page, looking for mistakes you might have missed. As a magazine editor, I work with about ten proofreaders for every issue. It never fails that each will find a mistake everyone else missed. The more eyes reviewing your site, the better.

Make sure search engines will direct traffic to your Web site.

Unless you intend to direct all traffic to your site through your own efforts, you will want to be found by the search engines. Companies spend thousands of dollars to improve their Web site's ranking. This is important because a higher ranking provides increased credibility and traffic. To improve your ranking, you'll need to consider relevance, uniqueness, and age of the site content; accessibility of documents on your site; effective use of keywords and other HTML tags; and how many other Web sites link to yours. Search engine optimization companies provide consultation (for a price) to make sure your site shows up on the search engine radars.

Web Forums

Imagine a gathering of hundreds of individuals all interested in the same topic, asking questions and sharing their experiences. If these people were in the same room, it would be chaotic. The conversations would be deafening and people would bump into each other trying to find the person who held the answer to their specific question. However, the Web offers these gatherings every day in an organized system called a forum.

A Web forum might be called a discussion group, message board, or bulletin board, but the purpose of each is the same: to link together people with common interests. There is no special software required to access these forums, just your everyday Internet browser. Some are found as a component of a Web site.

Their format is very simple. As a user of the forum, you can start a thread which may be a comment, question, or other type of message. When you "post" your thread, other users reply to it and an online discussion begins. Many forums ask you to register and provide an email address, while others allow you to be anonymous. Some forums allow advanced use only by qualified individuals, such as professionals in the field that's the topic of the forum. An administrator oversees each forum to assure the discussion doesn't disintegrate or go off topic.

Forums serve a variety of purposes. Once you find a few that fit your needs, you can become a regular visitor. By posting different questions, you'll get diverse and creative solutions to your problems. By watching other discussions, your creativity might be sparked and you'll generate new business ideas, approaches, and models for yourself. If you are open to critique, forums provide excellent peer review opportunities. Just list your Web site address, or ideas, and ask for input.

In addition to providing knowledge and encouragement, forums can establish you as an expert in your field. Many forums allow you to put your Web site in your signature. As you answer the questions of others, you'll generate interest in who you are and what you do. Over time, you'll become recognized as a professional who knows her stuff. For example, if you run a graphic design service from home and offer others free advice or solve problems, you are demonstrating your expertise and promoting your business in the best way possible.

Finding the right forum for you will take some research. A good place to start is by asking friends, business associates, and other home-based workers in your field. Tod has gotten lots of Web site technical advice through Y!Stores, our Web site host. Most of the large search engine Web sites, such as Google and MSN, sponsor forums. To find a group with your specific interest, a search engine can help start your search. Type in the topic and key phrase "discussion group." Another good approach is to go through a reputable Web site.

A few Web sites I can recommend for forums on working at home or finding jobs include Transition Home (www.transitionhome .org), Christian Work at Home Moms (www.cwahm.com); Work at Home Moms (www.wahm.com); and Telecommuting Moms (www.telecommutingmoms.com). Crosswalk.com offers an extensive list of general Christian discussion groups.

For small business owners, the right discussion group offers you large company resources, expert knowledge, and an opportunity to market yourself as an expert.

Email Marketing

Just the other day, I got an email from one of my favorite stores telling me about an exclusive online sale. The message prompted me to visit the Web site to review the store's clearance items. Unfortunately, they didn't have the exact item I wanted, or they would have made a sale. But they might have what I want next time they email me.

Email marketing is estimated to be a multibillion-dollar-per-year industry. Ministries and for-profit companies send informational newsletters, notices of sales, and announcements of new products. The advantages are obvious to the business owner. It's relatively inexpensive—no postage, production, or supply costs. It's fast—the business can deliver the message instantaneously. And the sender can easily track the results of the campaign. The disadvantages are that it can be perceived as spam (junk mail) and doesn't always have the same impact as published material.

This marketing approach is easily incorporated into your business plan. You'll need to choose an email software, which should be offered by your Web host. Your monthly fee will depend on how many emails you send a month. Yahoo.com charges $10 a month for 500 emails. Any program you choose should include the following components:

- Easy-to-create HTML templates
- Personalization ability
- Opt-in builder
- Automated subscribe/unsubscribe
- Preview and test message capability
- Tracking capabilities
- Compliance with antispam regulations

First, create a mailing list.

To put together your mailing list, start with your friends, family, and existing customers. Incorporate a newsletter subscription or mailing list opt-in section on every page of your Web site. Make sure it's clear what your customers will receive when they sign up. To increase your mailing list, use incentives such as exclusive discounts to members. To avoid unhappy customers, or worse, annoyed friends, make sure the unsubscribe option is conspicuous and easy to use.

Then target your email's content and design so that both will interest your customer.

Before you jump on the email marketing bandwagon, make sure you know what you will send to your customers. The best public relations approach is to provide useful information in significantly greater proportion to your sales pitch. Almost every businessperson has knowledge that will benefit someone else. Put it down in writing and share it through your newsletter. If you are starting a children's party business, then send out tips on how to host all types of parties. A makeup consultant can write about skin care. If your writing skills are weak, consider soliciting the help of a friend. Remember, with practice, you will improve.

In the design of your email, use your company logo and deliver a consistent look. If you want the reader to purchase something as part of your marketing plan, then include a clear call to action. You can also include a teaser note with a link back to your Web site. If you do so, direct the reader to the right page, not just the home page. Allow the recipient to read material as either HTML or text. Finally, develop a consistent delivery plan, such as quarterly or monthly.

Tracking results will tell you if this is an effective marketing tool for your business. Your software should be able to easily provide the following statistics:

- Openings—how many people opened the email
- Bounce-backs—no longer valid email addresses
- Responses—how many readers emailed you back
- Click-throughs—how many of them actually visited the Web site

As you experiment with an email campaign, keep track of revenue changes related to the effort. If you aren't seeing an increase in sales or business, perhaps it's not the right marketing avenue for your business. If that's the case, drop it after a year and put your energies into something else.

Article Submissions

If you are a business owner with any writing skill, you simply must consider article submissions in your marketing plan. Web sites everywhere are looking for high-quality, informative articles to include in their libraries or archives. This is an absolutely free way to promote your business and establish yourself as an expert through your bio at the end of the article. Additionally, by including a link back to your Web site in your bio, you can dramatically increase your search engine ranking as people visit your site.

Most Web sites include writer's guidelines. Start a file of Web sites that would potentially accept your articles and print their guidelines. As you write articles, refer to the guidelines to make sure you meet the Web site's requirements. Editors won't consider a 1,000-word article if their guidelines ask for 500-word articles. Find other people to critique your article before submitting it. It still needs to be well-written to be accepted.

The first place to put articles is on your own enewsletter or blog. Then submit to specific, industry-related Web sites—especially to those that you like and visit often. There are also general information article directories, such as goarticles.com. Homebiztools.com offers a long list of article directories. Click on Resources then Article Directories.

Editors across the world are looking for free articles to include on their own sites, or to quote experts. As we increasingly look to the Internet for our information, articles by experts will grow in importance.

Weblogs (Blogs)

Chances are you have a friend who has set up a blog and is faithfully writing her thoughts on life. A good friend whose husband was transferred to Germany set one up to post photos and stories about their time overseas. The blog saves her from writing letters every month and sending photos of the kids to grandparents.

A blog is basically a mini Web site, populated with the site owner's personal opinions—much like a diary. The difference is you are publishing your diary to thousands (millions?) of potential readers who are able to not only read your inner thoughts, but respond to them as well.

Once you've registered your blog with a service (like blogger .com or typepad.com), you start writing, press a button, and you're a published author. According to Eponym, a blogging Web site, recent US studies have found that about 1 in 20 people already has a blog, and 1 in 6 people reads them.

Blogs are now being used by businesses to market their services or products. Some of the potential benefits of maintaining a blog include:

- Puts a personality behind a name. Business on the Internet is a very impersonal approach. A blog can help your customers get to know you and feel better about doing business with you.
- Improves your customer service. You can express personal thoughts about your product or service.
- Increases traffic to your Web site. Search engines send spiders out looking for new content. The more new stuff you add to your blog, the greater your chances of rising in the rankings. Just make sure the new content you add has got some meat in it. Random ramblings don't excite many potential customers.

Pay Per Click

We've all seen pay-per-click (PPC) ads when we've done a search. They're on the top or side of the search page, and usually say something like "sponsored link." They contain a headline, a short description, and a link to a Web site. In fact, they also can be found in a variety of different Web sites. Why are they there and how did they get there?

PPC ads are one more way to drive customers to your Web site and, as the name implies, you only pay when someone clicks on your link. The hope is they will become a customer after reviewing your incredible site.

The process is relatively simple. First decide how your customers will likely look for you. Will they be looking for a brand-name product you sell or perhaps a service, such as editing? As a simplistic example, let's say you sell Mary Engelbreit teacups (like we do). We might decide to place a PPC ad on one of the three main search engines: Google, MSN, or Yahoo! We would agree to pay a placement fee for either a key word (teacups) or products (Mary Engelbreit teacups).

When someone makes a search for Mary Engelbreit teacups, voilà, there we are. When a visitor clicks on our PPC ad, we are charged a fee. You can control the amount you spend by setting a daily limit for each of your accounts. PPC ads have a conversion rate of 2 percent to 8 percent. While they can bring a good flow of traffic to your site, you still have the job of making the final sale. Also, you are monitored to see how much traffic you get. If you aren't a moneymaker for the search engine, you will likely be asked to leave.

The frustrating part of this chapter is I was only able to touch the surface of the Internet. It's a wild ride out there on the information superhighway. As overwhelming as it seems, we cannot ignore its potential or its dangers. The best approach is to address one topic at a time and go deeper through your own research. When you've mastered one topic, then move on. Then, in a few years when the Internet has reinvented itself, call me and we'll have a good laugh at how antiquated this chapter is.

CHAPTER 14

• • • • • • • •

SETTING UP A HOME OFFICE

My second job out of college was for a developer of retirement and assisted-living communities. The CEO of the company, Prill Kuhn, was a woman with a passion for developing beautiful living communities for seniors. While she abided by all the right code restrictions and architectural guidelines, she pushed the envelope to make them lovely.

Prill always imagined her mother walking the hallways or sitting in the dining room. Where would she rest and what would she gaze upon as she got her mail? These types of questions guided her philosophy of blending function and grace.

One of her pet peeves was cluttered-looking administrative offices. While people at other companies might tape notes to walls or windows, we put them in picture frames. We drank our sodas out of a glass and never ate at our desk. Clutter was abhorred and order was the rule of the day.

I learned a lot from Prill. When she was in town, she'd walk with the management staff around the community and share her philosophy on caring for the aging and creating a beautiful home for them. One such walk sticks out in my mind. It was the day my approach to organization changed forever.

As we walked around the administrative offices, Prill shared tips on how to keep our workspaces attractive and clutter free. She chatted about options and warned us, with great concern, to stay away from the cereal-box-on-top-of-the-refrigerator syndrome. I sucked in my breath, wondering if someone told her about my house. That's exactly where my cereal boxes were that day, and had been for years.

I mused about her comment for days; alternately defending my approach (they don't all fit in my small cupboards) and considering options (I could put them in storage containers that do fit in my cupboards). Needless to say, the cereal boxes came down, I scrubbed the top of the refrigerator, and I positioned a plant in an attractive pot in place of cardboard.

The point of her comment was to put a little extra effort into organization so that it also looks nice. While I don't pour my sodas into goblets anymore, I have incorporated Prill's concern for making practicality as pretty as possible in my home, including my office.

Because you'll be spending hours each week at your workspace, we'll take some time in this chapter to explore ways to make it a productive and inspiring area.

Make It Work for You

Few home-workers have the luxury of creating a private office. Most of us carve out a corner of the living room or family room for our workspace. In very small spaces, a kitchen table might double as your desk. Your home is what it is. It may not be perfect, but don't waste time or mental energy fussing over what you can't change right now. Instead, consider how you can enhance it with some minor changes.

When I first started working at home, I set up a desk in an upstairs guest bedroom. It was away from the hubbub of the household yet overlooked the backyard, where I could supervise play from a distance. The quiet of the room was great, but its distance from the family caused problems.

First, I only went up to work when I knew I had an uninterrupted block of time. Since that didn't happen often, I found myself procrastinating. Then, when I did go upstairs, minor interruptions took more time. If someone came to the door or I had to transfer clothes to the dryer, it took more effort to get back into the swing of work.

My other problem involved unsupervised children in the kitchen and family room. Being distanced from the action, I often found myself walking downstairs to check on a noise, or lack of noise. Open chip bags, cookie crumbs on the carpet, and soda cans on the counter aren't big problems, but they were frustrating to me.

According to the "experts," my old office was in a perfect location. It was quiet, had a door I could shut, and was big enough to accommodate my files and desk. However, it didn't work for me. I've since learned that each of us needs to determine how and when we work best, and allow our office needs to flow from there.

As odd and unpractical as it sounds, I now have my desk in the middle of the action and love it. There was an empty niche under our stairs where we had tucked an unplayed piano. We bit the bullet, paid to have the piano moved upstairs, and built a desk and cabinets into the space. The built-ins coordinate with the kitchen so it looks more like furniture than an office.

My best work is done when our kids are at school or playing at a friend's house, and more mindless tasks can be done when everyone is home. It's easy to check emails or finish a project when I only have small bites of time available. And I can oversee the kitchen, backyard, and front door in a glance. In other words—no more excuses.

As you consider your space options, think about your personality, your privacy needs, and the makeup of your family. Get creative by rearranging furniture, redoing a closet, or converting an armoire. If you know you'll need more space or will be meeting privately with clients, you might invest in converting a portion of your garage, basement, or attic into an office. Adding on to your home is also an option. However, before making any structural or use changes, check with your homeowners association and city codes.

Another consideration for choosing an office space is whether or not you will use it exclusively for your business. If the answer is yes, ask your accountant about IRS deductions. If you never use your desk for personal reasons, this might warrant a separate space.

One last thought is to stay out of your bedroom if possible. You will need a haven to retreat from work. Plus, if you have any trouble falling asleep or waking in the middle of the night, the last thing you want to see when you open your eyes is a pile of work.

Make It Functional

Having the proper supplies is more than half the battle to begin and successfully complete a project. Nothing is more frustrating (besides telemarketing calls) than needing a file folder and not having one.

Organization is the key to making your workspace functional. I find that order refreshes my creativity and productivity, while clutter drains. Investing time setting up an organized office will pay off exponentially in the future. Statistics reveal the average executive spends 150 hours a year searching for lost documents, and a moderately disorganized person loses about 2 hours every day due to disorder. This inspires me to pursue greater functionality and order.

Here are some things you might want to consider:

Filing system. This could be your strongest tool for staying on top of your workload. I find that my piles of paper grow because I don't know where to store what's in them. A good filing system is the answer.

As space allows, purchase the largest and sturdiest filing cabinet you can. Make sure it has at least two drawers, and stay away from the cheapest option. The glides may work now, but envision it filled with files.

Then, purchase a large supply of hanging folders and manila file folders and keep them in the front of your filing cabinet. Productivity expert David Allen recommends adding a label maker to your office product list. In his book *Getting Things Done*

Allen writes, "Typeset labels change the nature of your files and your relationship to them. . . . It makes it fun to open the drawer to find or insert things."

One philosophy of filing is to group like files in broad categories. Label the hanging folders *Insurance, Equipment, Current Projects,* and so on. Within each category, alphabetize your files. Or, you can avoid labeling the hanging folders altogether and just put files in alphabetical order.

Once you've decided on your system, keep from overstuffing your file drawers. Jam-packed drawers will discourage you from daily filing or creating new files. Consider your files as an integral part of your home office, and invest in additional ones when necessary. Purging your files every 6 to 12 months is a good practice.

Supplies. Keep your office stocked with all the doodads you'll need to produce a professional product. Your initial tendency may be to avoid purchasing duplicate items to those you already own. However, you'll waste time and energy walking to the kitchen every time you need scissors or tape. Maintaining a well-stocked desk is a time-saver and, consequently, a money-saver.

These may seem like no-brainers, but here's a list of items you may want to keep handy:

- Scissors
- Ruler
- Binder clips
- Staple remover
- Hole punch
- Pencils
- Highlighters
- Index cards
- Paper shredder
- Notecards for personal notes
- Tape
- Paper clips
- Stapler
- Pens
- Pencil sharpener
- Markers
- Sticky notes
- Stamps
- Stationery

Electronic needs. With the rapid speed of change in the technology field, this section will probably be outdated by the time it's in print. To become better educated, spend some time in an electronics store talking with an employee who loves his or her job. Of course, the employee's goal is to get you to buy the store's products, so listen with that in mind.

You'll want to consider a computer that will support the type and amount of work you'll do. Since most home-based work is Internet-based, arrange for the fastest speed Internet service available in your area. This will save you an indeterminate amount of time and money in the future.

Will you need a fax machine, scanner, or photo printer? What about a binding system or a laminator? Evaluate your needs and invest in the highest quality product you can afford. Check with your accountant on whether these items can be deducted as business expenses.

Make It Safe

For years I suffered with a sharp pain in my left shoulder blade after working for a few hours. Assuming it was a normal part of typing for a living, I took breaks, got back rubs, and accepted the minor pain.

It wasn't until my sister Liz, a purchaser for a major university, commented on the importance of ergonomics that I put two and two together. I was using the only desk we had at the time, and it wasn't designed for a computer. That meant the keyboard and mouse sat too high. Consequently I held my shoulders up and my arms were at the wrong angle. Because I'm left-handed, my left shoulder blade hurt. Now that my keyboard is at a safe height, I type pain free.

Without a corporate human resource department to watch out for potential Occupational Safety and Health Administration (OSHA) violations, the home-worker can easily overlook the real physical dangers that can happen while working. Here are some safety details you might want to consider as you create your home office:

Glare. Watch for direct and reflected glare on your monitor screen. If you find yourself tilting your head to see the screen, you have a problem. To avoid this, invest in a glare-free monitor and close the blinds on windows.

Monitor height. To avoid other eyestrain issues, minimize the contrast between your screen and the background. Although facing a window can offer a lovely view, the bright background will cause problems.

Consider putting your monitor against a wall. Position the top of the monitor at about the same height or lower than your eyes and at least 18 to 24 inches from your face. If you can place your monitor further away and still read it, that's even better.

Chair. Consider a chair that allows for a slight recline. The ergonomics consulting company Ankrum Associates recommends "the idea of a much wider hip angle, with 130 degrees or so as an 'optimum' angle. The reason? When the hips are straightened, the vertebrae of the lower spine are aligned with each other in a way that reduces and evens out pressure on the intervertebral discs. Further, sitting upright is less desirable than reclining. When reclining, the lower back muscles work less and the spine supports less weight, since body weight is held up by the chair's backrest."

Shoulders, arms, and hands. Keep your elbow angle at 90 to 100 degrees as you work with the keyboard, keeping your arms held close to your sides. Keep your wrists flat when you are typing. Consciously relax your shoulders and arms. Keep the mouse and keyboard as close together as possible to eliminate unnecessary reaching. A chair with adjustable armrests is a great investment.

Breaks. Break up your work with frequent breaks and movement. UCLA's Ergonomics Department advises us to "take short 1–2 minute stretch breaks every 20–30 minutes. After each hour of work, take a break or change tasks for at least 5–10 minutes." Raise your arms, reposition your legs, or just stand up to eliminate the stress on your body.

Please don't ignore early warning signs of possible workplace trauma. Watch for persistent pain, tingling, numbness, burning, or aching. You may experience these signs all the time or after certain activities. First, consider the ergonomics of your home office and make changes when necessary. However, if the pain persists after making changes, visit a health professional.

Make It Beautiful

There's no reason our work areas shouldn't be functional and pleasing. As my boss taught me years ago, beauty is often in the details. As you approach your desk each day, consider which minor and major details you can change to perk up your space.

Clean up clutter. The absolute cheapest and quickest way to beautify your home office is to clean up the mess. There are lots of tips on overcoming clutter, but the best overall advice I can give you is for everything to have a place, and to be in its place. Clutter accumulates because we don't know what to do with it—it's that simple.

Spend some time going through every piece of paper and item on, under, beside, and above your desk. Ask yourself these questions. Can I . . .?

- file it? (important stuff)
- throw it away? (junk)
- give it away? (books and magazines you'll never read again)
- tuck it in a drawer? (stapler, pens)
- put it in a bookcase? (binders, notebooks)
- store it in a basket or decorative container? (sticky notes, paper clips)
- put it in another room? (seldom referenced books)
- replace it with something pretty? (attractive lamp, fabric-covered garbage can)
- hide it behind something? (cords)

Once you've answered these questions, start by tossing, shredding, or recycling unnecessary items. Put other items where they belong. If storage is an issue, make a house-hunting/shopping list. Search your home for attractive accessories to decorate your office.

Arrange for adequate storage space. Inadequate storage space is almost always a problem. We just need to get creative while at the same time remembering how it looks. Can you convert a hall closet into a storage space for your work? Or invest in furniture that does double duty, like a coffee table with drawers or baskets?

Other attractive storage options include fabric-covered boxes, fabric-lined baskets, wicker baskets, or boxes. Consider stacking wicker files boxes on the floor with books and a lamp on top.

Use color that energizes and cheers you. Incorporate color in obvious and not-so-obvious places. Consider painting a wall or stenciling a border around your desk. Bring in color by recovering the upholstery on your chair or using a slipcover. Add a lamp with an attractive shade. Sew a fabric cover to hide your printer while turned off. Look at your home office as an opportunity to decorate, and I believe you'll be inspired.

Choose creative, yet practical accessories. Although we are trying to reduce the clutter, a few well-placed accessories will enhance your desk. Just because our work is business oriented doesn't mean we can't add a touch of elegance and fun. Consider incorporating some treasured items, like teacups or a lovely vase. Fill it with fresh flowers and add a candle (away from paper, of course).

Add whimsy by using conventional items in unconventional ways. Cooking fans could use muffin tins to hold small items or a kitchen utensil holder to store pens and scissors. What about using some vintage tin canisters or measuring cups for storage? Decorative shelving options, like a black wire spice rack or shabby-chic shelf, can provide storage while adding to your new look.

Making your home office beautiful doesn't need the advice of a professional designer; it just takes looking at it with new eyes and considering creative options.

Make It Inspiring

It's easy to be so buried in the day-to-day necessities of working from home that we neglect to feed our souls. Look for little ways to remind yourself of your value to God, your high calling as a woman, and your purpose for the day. This might be found in a print from a Christian bookstore or a plaque with a favorite Scripture verse. To keep the cost down, ask your children to draw pictures for you and frame them.

Hang a photo collage filled with memories of time with family or places you love. When a deadline approaches, these photos will inspire you to press on.

Another way to bring God's Word into your workday is by subscribing to a free devotional. Proverbs 31 offers a devotion written specifically for women every weekday, sent directly to your email address. You can subscribe online at www.proverbs31. org. Crosswalk.com offers an assortment of free devotions if this doesn't fit your needs.

When you need to rest your eyes from looking at your computer screen, consider writing a Scripture verse to memorize on an index card and looking at that. Here are some Scripture verses that inspire me when I need a touch from God's heart to mine.

"With your help I can advance against a troop; with my God I can scale a wall. As for God, his way is perfect; the word of the Lord is flawless. He is a shield for all who take refuge in him. For who is God besides the Lord? And who is the Rock except our God?" (2 Samuel 22:30–32).

"Therefore, if anyone is in Christ, he is a new creation; the old has gone, the new has come!" (2 Corinthians 5:17).

"Commit to the Lord whatever you do, and your plans will succeed" (Proverbs 16:3).

"Trust in the Lord with all your heart and lean not on your own understanding; in all your ways acknowledge him, and he will make your paths straight" (Proverbs 3:5–6).

"The Lord is compassionate and gracious, slow to anger, abounding in love. . . . For as high as the heavens are above the earth, so great is his love for those who fear him; as far as the east is from the west, so far has he removed our transgressions from us." (Psalm 103:8, 11).

"'For I know the plans I have for you,' declares the Lord, 'plans to prosper you and not to harm you, plans to give you hope and a future" (Jeremiah 29:11).

"I am focusing all my energies on this one thing: Forgetting the past and looking forward to what lies ahead" (Philippians 3:13 NLT).

"He is before all things, and in Him all things hold together" (Colossians 1:17).

CHAPTER 15

• • • • • • • •

BALANCING WORK AND HOME

Balancing the needs of our families, jobs, homes, and ministry seems a never-ending task. There's always someone who needs our help, an assignment that needs to be finished, and laundry that piles up. I once seriously considered asking my family if they would wear the same clothes for a week, just so I could catch up.

Finding balance is one of the top hurdles we face in life. It's like we're those Pokey and Gumby dolls, whose arms, legs, and heads can get stretched in multiple directions. Although those rubber dolls can't break, sometimes we do break from the strain of demanding responsibilities.

I learned a lot about balance, or the lack of it, in a step aerobics class. My family had moved to North Carolina, and it was the first time in my adult life I hadn't worked outside my home. With extra time on my hands, I joined the YMCA determined to get in shape. I started on the elliptical machine, and after six months I figured I was ready for the next level of exercise, which in my mind was a beginning step class. What I've since learned is they need a "sub-beginner" class for some of us.

The first class started out fine. I was enjoying the music, the pace was slow, and I could understand the leader's directions. I was stepping up and to the left, and I even figured out the grapevine step. But as the music accelerated, so did our steps, and so did my heart rate. Just when I'd mastered the basic steps, the teacher had us do something fancy. With our hands on our hips, we took a little hop and landed with our right toe pointed forward, then left, then right, then left. We alternated our feet faster and faster.

For the briefest of moments, I felt like a graceful Irish step dancer in *Riverdance*, with Michael Flatley by my side. I actually maintained the pace for a few seconds, but then made a grave tactical error when I looked down to admire my fast-moving feet. Doing so, my betraying appendages flew out from under me, while my arms flailed in circles as I desperately tried to regain my balance. All the arm-flapping in the world didn't help as I tumbled to the ground, flat on my bottom.

I wasn't hurt, and hoped to quietly and quickly rejoin the class . . . but that was not to be. The petite, fit leader on the microphone kindly asked: "Did you just fall? Are you OK?" However, in my mind it sounded like a slow and extremely loud bullhorn: D–i-i-i-i-d-d-d-d Y-o-o-o-o-u-u-u-u J-u-u-u-u-s-s-s-t-t-t F-a-a-a-l-l-l-l? A-a-a-a-a-r-r-r-r-e-e-e-e Y-o-o-o-o-u-u-u-u O-O-O-O-O-K-K-K-K-K?

I lumbered up, my pride stinging, and nodded yes, as every lovely southern head in the room turned to see my disgrace. Skulking out of the room wasn't an option and I finished the class, albeit more cautiously.

That day in the gym I was thrown off balance by trying to do more than I was able and by taking my eyes off the instructor. I wanted to keep up with the crowd, but I just couldn't do it. Just like falling in a step class, our lives can get off balance too.

One of the most effective ways to live a balanced life is to keep your eyes focused on Jesus and to align your priorities with God's priorities. The problem is that many people have never identified their priorities, and even those who have sometimes don't make life choices that reflect them.

Keep Your Eyes on Jesus

During the aerobics class, I should have watched the instructor instead of my feet. Then I could have matched my step to hers. With my eyes forward, my balance would have been maintained. To keep balance in life, I need to keep my eyes on Jesus as the center of my existence.

Why should Jesus be the center of our life? The Scriptures tell us that Jesus holds all things together. Colossians 1:16–17 says, "For by him all things were created: things in heaven and on earth, visible and invisible, whether thrones or powers or rulers or authorities; all things were created by him and for him. He is before all things, and in him all things hold together." The converse truth in this passage is that without Jesus, all things fall apart, including our lives.

As I pattern my step to His, my life takes on balance. As I align my priorities to His, I find a graceful flow to my life. Once my eyes are firmly on Jesus, I won't try to keep up with those around me. My pace will be set according to my abilities and what God is calling me to do.

Identify Your Priorities

Once my eyes are focused on Jesus, then I need to be clear on the things that should take top priority in my life. If you aren't sure about your priorities, ask yourself these questions:

1. What can only I do? (Only I can develop my faith, take care of my health, be my husband's wife, and be my three sons' mother.)
2. What has God entrusted to me? (God has entrusted me with the care of a home, the care of children, my health, and the management of my time and money, to name a few.)
3. Am I a good steward of what I already have? (Do I manage money well? Do I care for my home? Do I love my husband and children the way I should? Do I work as effectively as I can?)
4. What passion has God put in my heart? (I have a passion for helping children and youth come to love Jesus and for women to draw closer to God and align their lives with His will.)

5. What has God asked you to do that you haven't done yet? (For years I knew God was calling me to write, but I did nothing about it.)

Order your priorities.

Once you've identified your priorities, list them in order of importance. Then, allocate the number of hours each week you devote to each one. If you're like most of us, you'll find your priorities and time are out of balance. The things you value most get the least amount of your time and often the lowest amount of energy and enthusiasm.

Make tough decisions.

When you have identified your priorities, then make changes in your life to increase your effectiveness in these areas. This most certainly will involve sacrifice, sometimes even of things you enjoy doing. And it will definitely involve pruning. Only you can make the tough decisions necessary to live a balanced life.

In *The Purpose-Driven Life*, Rick Warren writes, "If you want your life to have impact, focus it! Stop dabbling. Stop trying to do it all. Do less. Prune away even good activities and do only that which matters most."

What responsibilities in your life, even good things, keep you from being effective in what matters most? This is a hard question to answer because it may mean giving up things you love to do. But we have to address this question, as the answer will guide our pruning.

Beginning to work from home will definitely involve pruning. I thought I'd have all kinds of extra time, but I was wrong. I do have greater flexibility to focus on my top priorities, but I don't have time to add lots of new responsibilities. I learned that the hard way by jumping into things, and then had to slowly prune wonderful activities from my life.

Finding balance in your life might take time. Some things you can prune immediately, while others may take time to fulfill a commitment. However, if you discover your life is out of balance in one area, start making changes immediately. By delaying, you'll find your effectiveness hindered in almost every other area of your life. Why? Because your priorities are not in alignment with God's priorities for you.

A life with priorities out of God's order is like driving on a tire with a bald spot or trying to steer a car that's out of alignment. The car may keep running, but that one area out of alignment affects all other areas. And has the potential to do serious damage if not addressed and repaired.

My husband is a runner. After running his first marathon Tod had a problem with his foot. After every run, short or long, his foot would hurt horribly. Bags of ice and ibuprofen sustained his training, but then his knee started hurting and his hip started hurting. After 18 months of pain he broke down and went to the doctor.

After a few x-rays they told him his knee and his hip looked normal, but his foot looked broken. A referral to a specialist showed he actually had tendonitis. He was fitted for orthotics and now runs pain free.

The root of the problem with his knee and his hip was his foot. Because he favored his foot, it threw his knee and hip out of alignment. This is like a life with priorities out of God's alignment. It throws the rest of our life out of balance.

Find Balance Between Your Work and Your Life

With any new venture, such as working from home, you'll need to readjust your commitments to accommodate the change. Following are some specific tips on how to balance many of the responsibilities women face while working at home.

Schedule daily time alone with God.

Our time alone with God in prayer and reading His Word is our source of necessary inspiration. However, for many of us, this time falls to the bottom of our priority lists as the demands of the day. A great idea for making this jump to the top of the list is to approach it like we would a meeting with our boss. Author Tracey Russell shared this tip in an article entitled "The Staff Meeting." Tracey explained, "One day I heard my mentor, Sandy, describe her quiet time as a 'staff meeting' with God. Suddenly, I felt God opening my heart to use meeting principles to approach quiet time with Him. With Sandy's help, we developed four staff meetings principles with a spiritual basis: preparation, perspective, personal application, and praise for productivity."

In her daily "staff meeting," Tracey incorporates a time of preparing her heart through prayer and then hearing the "Boss's" perspective on life through reading Scripture and listening for His voice. The next step involves personal application. Tracey advises, "Personal application of God's Word requires us to process what we have read and use it in our daily life. We are literally discussing with God how He wants to direct us in light of His truth for that day." Take time to write down areas God may be calling you to change. Finally, spend time praising God for all He's done in your life.

For those of us who are comfortable in the corporate world, this is one way to spend time with God in a style we know. God longs to give us direction and wisdom for our day. Make this a priority and incorporate your business planning into this time.

"Show me your ways, O Lord, teach me your paths; guide me in your truth and teach me, for you are God my Savior" (Psalm 25:4–5).

Make your calendar your friend.

Cindy Hope Harrell, a Charlotte realtor and *Southern Living* Home representative, advises, "Schedule everything, including time with your family. You simply have to consistently prioritize your day and be intentional in what you do."

Now that you're home, you still need some type of calendar to schedule important activities. To make sure you leave room for the important things in life, put those on the calendar first. That might mean your quiet time with God, lunch with your mom, a Bible study, or your son's football practice. Schedule whatever is important to you, including time for yourself.

Wisely integrate work and home.

There's a reality of working at home. As hard as you try, it's difficult to draw firm dividing lines. Lynda Evans, a home-based entrepreneur, offers this advice: "The greatest thing I've learned is you cannot separate what you do from your home, everything blends. To be successful as an entrepreneur it needs to be part of your life and your family's life. If you have a dream and a goal, your family has to be incorporated into that. That way, we all know which way we are going. Together we ask, 'Where do we want to be next year?'"

This attitude helps to overcome the guilt you may have if you need to leave the house for work or you have to arrange child care during the day. Your work isn't something you do on your own. It also helps your children feel more a part of your life.

Set boundaries you won't cross.

There's a healthy balance to be found in integrating your work and home, yet not being dominated by the demands of work. In order to keep your priorities in line and hang onto your sanity, identify those boundaries you won't cross. For some that means not taking phone calls at night or working on certain days.

Victoria Atkinson, an Arbonne International consultant, shares, "I will never book a party on a Saturday because that is our family day. Even if it means losing a party, I feel God will honor my faithfulness of putting my family first. And of course I don't do any business on Sundays." Shari Braendel is a public speaker and Mary Kay consultant who begins her day at 10:00 in the morning so she can spend early morning hours with her children.

Another way to prevent the phone from being a problem is to add a second line with an answering machine or voice mail. That way, you can receive business calls, record messages professionally, and answer them when you have time.

Multitask when you can.

There are tasks that need our full attention. For those that don't, try doing two things at once. A phone headset is a great investment for light conversations or those times when we're put on hold and need free hands to type, cook, or clean.

Maureen Poirier, a Creative Memories and Reliv consultant, finds multitasking to be a great help in finding balance. A few examples from Maureen's life include listening to tapes while she's housecleaning and driving, having kids help with the care of the house, and grouping errands.

Implement Wise Ways to Work with Children at Home

For many of us, our children are why we work from home. The truth is, as much as we love being near our sweet kids, they can make home-based work challenging. Depending on the age and personality of your children, you'll need to plan creatively so they feel like a blessing, not a bother.

Invest in independent activities.

Before you plop Johnny in front of a television set, spend some time shopping for mind-enriching activities he can do alone. The library, teacher supply stores, educational toy stores, and craft supply stores are great places to find activities. Just as a teacher plans his or her day, plan your child's day with things he or she can do. Offer your child a variety of activities to break up the time.

A second computer might also be a good investment. You can have "work" time together with your child using computer programs you've selected.

Have clear rules.

Make sure your children know the rules about how to act when you are working. If they have a question, let them know the appropriate way to ask it. Running into the room shouting would be unacceptable. Walking up and quietly putting a hand on your shoulder might be a better alternative. Let kids know what problems they should interrupt you for and what they should handle alone. Anticipating situations and defining appropriate behavior should help alleviate many issues. We've found that writing and posting the rules helps with school-age children.

One of the hardest things on children is surprise discipline.

When we get upset over something they've done but we haven't told them it's wrong, we need to share the burden. Think through possible problem scenarios, options for dealing with them, and consequences if children break the rules. Preannounce this information and follow through with consequences if necessary.

Set a work schedule.

C. J. Hayden, author of *Get Hired Now!* and *Get Clients Now!* writes, "Setting regular working hours will help you manage your time better as well as give some guidelines to your family. Build your hours around the family activities that are important to you. If your kids get home at 2:00, for example, set up your work day from 8:30 to 2:00 and 4:00 to 6:00." C. J. suggests changing your schedule when necessary and posting your work hours for others to see.

For very small children and babies, a better plan might be to work around their schedules. Do your focused work while they are sleeping.

Hire care when needed.

There may be times when hired child care is needed. Use this time wisely. Although it may be tempting to run errands, spend this time doing work that requires a deeper level of attention.

Join or start a babysitting co-op.

When we moved to North Carolina, I was blessed to move into a neighborhood with a preexisting babysitting co-op. There were eight or ten other moms with preschool children who were part of the group. It was very organized, with each mom taking turns serving as secretary. We spent hours and earned hours depending on how many children we watched or how many of our own children were watched by others. This seemed more like a play day to my son because he got to spend time with his friends. If you have small children, consider starting something like this in your area. *Make sure you choose women you know and trust personally*. Never let strangers join the group.

Take frequent breaks.

Make sure you stop frequently and give your children undivided attention. When your child knows you are focused completely on her, a ten-minute break will help fill her "love tank" and her need to know you care. Make these breaks fun for both of you.

Have prearranged signals.

There are times when my kids walk into the room, unaware that I'm on the phone. Instead of putting the caller on hold, my kids know when I lightly snap my fingers it's time to quiet down. A mute button on your phone might also come in handy in these situations.

Take Care of Yourself

Make sure you take time to care for your spiritual, physical, and mental health. Without health in these areas, you will find yourself dragging. In Proverbs 31 there is a beautiful example of a home-based woman entrepreneur who modeled health. She made and sold linen garments and sashes, she bought a field, and planted a vineyard with her earnings. On top of all that, she oversaw the needs of her household with diligence. The chapter also gives us hints on how she handled her responsibilities with such grace.

Verse 17 reads, "She sets about her work vigorously; her arms are strong for her tasks." We see that the Proverbs 31 woman worked with strength and vigor. Because most of our work today is inactive, we must be committed to our health: getting sufficient sleep, eating a balanced diet, and maintaining appropriate weight and strong muscles. We should take time to care for our bodies so that we have the energy to address our responsibilities.

We also know she honored the Lord above all. Proverbs 31:30 tells us, "Charm is deceptive, and beauty is fleeting; but a woman who fears the Lord is to be praised." This isn't the fear we have when faced with danger, but the awe and respect for a God who is greater than we can imagine. When we have that much respect for Someone, His opinion matters more than anyone else's. And when God's opinion matters more to us than our mother's, our best friend's, or our neighbor's, we start getting our priorities straight in life and ultimately finding balance.

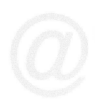

CHAPTER 16

· · · · · · · ·

EMOTIONAL CHALLENGES OF STAYING HOME

Once your dream to be home is fulfilled, the reality of life quickly sinks in. No more spur-of-the moment lunches out with co-workers, no one in the next office to brainstorm with, no reason to get dressed up. If there are small children at home, your change is even more drastic. Now you don't even get a bathroom break, and talking on the phone becomes a challenge.

Perhaps the most surprising part of the transition home is the emotional challenges you face. These may arise over time, and not everyone will face these challenges. But they are common to many.

This chapter discusses some of home-workers' basic emotional needs and how to address them once you are home.

Worth

Does what I do really matter? This may be a question most often asked by women and men who transition home to care for children and the home.

We live in a society that values success. But how do you define success in the intangible roles of spouse, parent, and homemaker?

Our culture is struggling to define the value of homemaking and parenthood, especially motherhood. At the turn of the twentieth century, there was significant pride involved in working at home. Women sought ways to improve their homemaking skills and learned about child-rearing from their mothers and families. The home was the center of the family.

The rise of industry sent many men away from the fields and into factories, while most women worked at home. The advent of war changed that dynamic, as men went to combat and women were needed to work the jobs that the men left vacant. After World War II, many women returned home and we had the idealized life of the 1950s. But some women discovered they liked working, which gave rise to the feminist movement of the 1960s. In the 1970s and 1980s lots of us tried to have it all. Now we are discovering that while we can try to have it all, there's a significant price to be paid.

Somehow, over time, we have devalued the roles of parent, spouse, and homemaker. Although we may speak of the importance of raising the next generation and having a strong family, our hearts are at odds with our words.

I confronted this reality when my youngest son "graduated" from kindergarten. At some point during the year the teachers had asked each child what he or she wanted to be when they grew up. Then, as the children's names were called to receive their diploma, each was introduced as "Robbie Whitwer, future policeman" and so on. I saw a shining glimpse of the future as each child proudly stepped up to the podium. There was nothing unusual until one little girl was introduced as a future mommy. Snickers coursed through the crowd, but my heart was deeply touched. Out of that entire class of children, only one saw motherhood as a career worth having.

Five years old is very young to be thinking about being a parent, husband, or wife, but the societal truth was revealed nevertheless.

We go to technical school, attend college for four years, sign up for professional seminars to pursue our career development—but how do we value and prepare for our lifelong roles?

When you start to feel insignificant, here are some tips to reinforce your value:

- Consider the difference you are making in the lives around you. Make a list of the impact being home has on those you love. Are you creating a peaceful home, providing children with protective oversight and training, offering full-time support of your spouse, honoring your parents?
- Create a job description. List skills and responsibilities you've acquired in your current role.
- Read through Scriptures that show your significance to God.

Individuality

Individuality is what makes you, you. So often we define ourselves by our external situations and behavior. When I worked I was creative, successful, well-liked, and organized.

We also define ourselves by what we do. You may introduce yourself as a writer, accountant, or teacher.

Take away the full-time career as you've always known it, and you may experience a loss of individuality. You may start to wonder, "Who am I really? I thought I knew once, but now I'm not sure."

What is the truth about your identity? Here are some truths you may already know, but it's good to reaffirm them.

1. You were created by God for a purpose.
2. You are imperfect, just as we all are, and need God's help.
3. You are deeply loved by the Creator of this universe.

When your confidence in your individuality starts to wane, here are two suggestions:

1. Get to know yourself. Get in touch with what you like, what makes you smile, what makes you sad. Incorporate your likes into your daily life.

2. Get to know God's view of you. Here are just a few Scripture verses that will help in this goal: Colossians 3:12 (we are chosen); Ephesians 1:3 (we are blessed); Ephesians 1:4 (we are in Christ); Ephesians 1:5 (we are adopted into God's family); 2 Corinthians 5:17 (we are a new creation).

Personal Development

When you stay home it's easy to serve others with such abandon that your own needs for personal development are ignored. Depending on the circumstances surrounding your transition home, you may find yourself putting your life on hold and delaying new opportunities.

Just because you are home doesn't mean your need for personal development has diminished. On the contrary, if you are assuming a new home-based career or investing more time in your family than ever before, your need for growth has actually increased. You are embarking on a new phase of life, which opens the door to a variety of opportunities to expand your knowledge and character.

In addition to personal growth, the Bible instructs us to "grow in the grace and knowledge of our Lord and Savior Jesus Christ" (2 Peter 3:18). If your spiritual growth is an area you have neglected in the past, commit to learning more about Christ.

Some other areas you may need to grow in include character development, homemaking skills, relationship skills, child development, financial management, and time management. Pick an area that could use improvement and commit to learning more.

Find an accountability partner to nudge you along the right path. Ecclesiastes 4:9–10 says, "Two are better than one, because they have a good return for their work: If one falls down, his friend can help him up. But pity the man who falls and has no one to help him up!" Share your need for development with a friend who will encourage you to continue if you start to stagnate.

Community

Loneliness is one of the most common complaints of being at home. God made us with a need for connection. In the workplace there is built-in sense of community. You're all in it together. It's where you belong and are needed. At home, you need to work at developing relationships.

Elisa Morgan and Carol Kuykendall in their book *What Every Mom Needs* define this need as intimacy. "Intimacy means 'Into-me-see.' When we are intimate with someone, we allow him to see into our character, our personhood. We become transparent and feel safe to admit our fears and longings."

What is intimacy? It isn't physical. It is that which characterizes one's deepest nature.

The best place to find intimacy is with your spouse. Often, when the kids arrive it's easy to stop investing in your marriage. And yet, God's design is for husband and wife to become one. When each spouse is pursuing a career, it's difficult to find time for dinner together, much less emotional intimacy.

As God directed me to put my marriage higher on my priorities, my relationship with my husband deepened. Our friendship has grown more in the time I've been home than in all the prior years.

Still, our spouse can't meet all our needs, so developing friends becomes important. My transition home was accompanied by a move across country, so finding a good friend who understood what I was experiencing was high on my priority list.

When I worked, my best friends were my co-workers. Once home, I discovered the task of finding friends became more challenging. It took work to develop good friendships, where in the workplace it happened naturally.

Here are some suggestions for finding friends:

- Volunteer. Volunteers often share common interests.
- Integrate friends into daily errands. Ask someone to drive around town with you as you complete your errands. It accomplishes a task and gives you time to talk.
- Plan special outings. One of my friends, Becky, is an expert at this. She is always coming up with a fun activity and asking a few friends to join her. Once we took a city bus downtown to a toy museum, and another time we went to a horse ranch to see newborn foals.
- Seek out people in your own situation. When my children

were small I had a radar for other mothers with small children. My best friendships were forged over Happy Meals.

- Be an inviter. Instead of waiting for others to approach you, take the initiative and invite someone over. It can be as simple as coffee or starting a Bible study. Here's the truth: Most of us are waiting at home for our phone to ring. If you wait for someone else to reach out, you'll languish at home.

Redefined Roles

When a spouse changes from a full-time job to no job or to a work-at-home job, there is a need to redefine the household roles. If these roles aren't discussed, there will be conflict and resentment.

Identify the household chores and who is responsible. When I stopped working, I took over the yard work. We had a big yard that took hours to maintain each week. Either I needed to take on this task during the week, or my husband would spend half of Saturday with the weed whacker and mower instead of with us. This would not have been possible if my children were younger, but mine were in school.

Expect that over time your new arrangements may need to be adjusted. You may think you will have lots of time to get things done. However, other commitments will arise now that you are home. It's human nature to underestimate how much time things will take. When my children were very small, I felt as if I just walked in circles some days. I was used to getting things accomplished at work, and could barely finish one task at home.

Be realistic about your available time, and openly discuss responsibilities with your family.

Know when to ask for help.

For many of us asking for help is a sign of weakness. This is especially true when you have worked outside the home. It's important to show you are invincible to employers.

Mothers often expect they can be all things to their children.

Unintentionally, a stay-at-home mother can shut out her husband from the care of the children. Mom may try to take care of the kids' needs before Dad gets home so the evening is more enjoyable. Then, when Mom does need help and her husband doesn't anticipate her needs, she can become resentful.

It's important to discuss your needs with your spouse in a healthy way. Be wise in your selection of time and use simple, direct, and kind words.

- Nonhealthy example: As soon as your spouse walks in the door you say: "These kids have been driving me crazy. It's your turn now!"
  Healthy example: This discussion would take place in a calm setting, away from the kids. "When you get home in the evening, would it be possible for you to spend some play time with the kids while I get dinner ready?
- Nonhealthy example: "I'm sick and tired of taking care of all this work around the house. No one appreciates me."
  Healthy example: "I'm having trouble keeping up with the laundry. Would you mind folding a couple of loads while you watch television?"

I have learned the truth of Proverbs 15:1: "A gentle answer turns away wrath, but a harsh word stirs up anger."

When your spouse does help, live with the results.

In my house, whoever replaces the toilet paper gets to pick which direction it goes. And if the whites get folded inside out, I don't "fix" them. When you show dissatisfaction with the help you get, you are less likely to get help again.

When I worked full-time, I had a boss who liked things done in a particular way. We worked together hosting special events, and often he would follow along behind me, resetting tables or changing decorations. His correction of me was defeating and little by little I just gave up trying. That's how your family feels when you redo their attempts to help. Sit on your hands or take a walk when the urge to "fix" hits.

Also, accept the fact that your spouse may not be able to help. This happens occasionally in my family, as my husband's job is demanding. If this is the case, then be understanding, resourceful, and look elsewhere for help.

Work out helping arrangements with your friends.

This is where a network of friends comes in handy. Remember that it blesses a friend to be able to help, just as much as the help blesses you. Another option is to barter, or trade, tasks. Perhaps you can mop your pregnant friend's floor and she can bake cookies for you. Join a support group such as MOPS (Mothers of Preschoolers) or set up a babysitting co-op.

Train your children to help.

As children get older, train them to help around the house. I have often underestimated my children's abilities, and hence missed out both on available help and on an opportunity for them to learn how to clean up after themselves and to feel like they matter to the family's well-being.

Finally, realize when you may need emotional help, and get it.

Depression is more common than most of us know. When you are home, you can hide from the world and cover up deep emotional hurts. Plus, there's this lie from the enemy that Christians should be able to handle everything with a happy smile. People buy into this lie and hide their true feelings.

If depression lasts more than a few days, seek counseling from your church or a Christian counselor. Emotional and psychological damage will bring long-term harm to you and your family.

Fun

When you are home, you may need to schedule time to have fun. Most people I know at home are very busy and find it difficult to take a break. This is especially true if you work from your home.

What are some ways you can meet your needs for fun?

Learn to play.

Play is something we do naturally as children, but as adults we may need to relearn it. Now we think of play as exercise, and so often avoid it. Invest in a bike, rollerblades, or basketball and get out and play.

Learn to laugh.

Having the wisdom to step back and see humor in a situation helps us gain control and gives us perspective. When you are home, it's all up to you. Your life can become very serious if you don't pursue laughter.

Slow down.

Savor where you are and find enjoyment in your new role at home. It takes discipline to see God's blessings when they are tucked into a busy day.

In his book *The Life You've Always Wanted,* John Ortberg identifies Americans as suffering from "hurry sickness." He explains, "One of the great illusions of our day is that hurrying will buy us more time." Ortberg goes on to pronounce, "The most serious sign of hurry sickness is a diminished capacity to love."

When I read those words, I was convicted. I knew I was guilty of conveying the strong message that I didn't have time for the small joys of friendship. Plus, how did my kids and husband feel as I flew past them accomplishing some "important" task?

Remember to slow down and enjoy life and those around you. A Christian is defined by love, and if hurrying keeps you from showing love, then, by all means, ruthlessly cut something from your schedule.

Hope

Despair is Satan's plan for you. You see, he has no hope and he wants Christians to join him in his pit of despair.

I guarantee you that at some point you will feel despair and hopelessness. Perhaps you'll think, "Why did I do this? This wasn't what I thought it would be."

But as a wise friend once told me, "Don't doubt in the dark what you know to be true in the light." In other words, if God has called you home, then He has a plan for you to fulfill.

Remember the words of Jeremiah 29:11: "'For I know the plans I have for you,' declares the LORD, 'plans to prosper you and not to harm you, plans to give you hope and a future.'"

While despair is Satan's plan for you, hope is God's design for you. There is only one place true hope can be found and that is in God. Hope comes in our relationship with Jesus and all our needs can be met completely and permanently.

Hope is what we hang onto when life doesn't make sense and tragedy hits. Hope is how we can agree with Paul and say, "And we know that in all things God works for the good of those who love Him, who have been called according to his purpose" (Romans 8:28).

Hope is how we endure when life is difficult. Paul, Silas, and Timothy wrote to the church of the Thessalonians and said, "We continually remember before our God and Father your work produced by faith, your labor prompted by love, and your endurance inspired by hope in our Lord Jesus Christ" (1 Thessalonians 1:3).

When you start to doubt your purpose at home, remember to look to God for the answers. Keep your eyes focused on Him, and He will direct your path.

CHAPTER 17
· · · · · · · ·

TIME MANAGEMENT AND ORGANIZATION TIPS

Time management is really self management. To manage someone or something means we can direct its behavior. Anyone who has ever tried to stretch one hour into two knows it can't be done. We can no more add an hour to our day than we can tell God what to do.

What we can do, however, is to make better choices on how we spend our time. It helps me better manage my time when I remember that it is a gift from God. Even though it's a gift, God does place some conditions on it. Just as with all of God's gifts, He expects us to use time wisely, to use it for His purposes, and give it away.

God wants us to start this pattern of giving by offering our gifts back to Him first, then to others. Not because God needs our money, homes, or time. But by offering our gifts back to God, we show that we trust Him to provide for our every need. We also show Him we surrender to His will in our lives.

Of all God's gifts, time may very possibly be the most valuable. The greatest acts of mercy, kindness, and boldness start with someone taking the time to make them happen. People are willing to pay thousands of dollars for time management seminars, organizational products, and services to figure out how to get more time in their life, or, at the very least, make the most of what they've got.

So the questions for today for each of us are these: What are we doing with the time we've got? Are we holding tightly to it, focusing on our time and desires? Or are we using it wisely to the glory of God?

Identify Time Wasters

To better manage our days, we should identify our most unproductive moments. Just like creating a financial budget to spot where we spend too much money or tracking everything we eat to determine our food weaknesses, a personal assessment of our day will reveal our time wasters.

It's very important to first address our weaknesses and bad habits before trying to implement new habits. Tod and I learned this lesson when we taught parenting classes at our church. We based the classes on the book *Willing Obedience* by William Richardson. Before delving into any child training techniques, Richardson teaches the three laws of learning. While these laws are presented in relation to child-rearing, I believe they can be applied to learning of any kind, including learning to be better stewards of our time.

The first law is "If it works, it happens again." The second is "Learning is a two-step." And the third law of learning states, "Small bites chew easier." The first and third are easily understood, but the second one needs a bit of explanation. Richardson writes, "Learning always involves two steps: stopping old behaviors, then starting new ones. . . . We must stop one comfortable behavior, such as lashing out in anger, in order to start a new foreign behavior, such as talking calmly about grievances." In order to get a better grip on using time wisely, we must stop or change those behaviors or circumstances that hinder our productivity.

While we all experience our unique set of time stealers, there are some common denominators. If you have trouble determining those that affect you most, consider this list prepared by the London-based company, Total Success Training:

- Interruptions—telephone
- Interruptions—personal visitors
- Meetings
- Tasks you should have delegated
- Procrastination and indecision
- Acting with incomplete information
- Dealing with team members
- Crisis management (firefighting)
- Unclear communication
- Inadequate technical knowledge
- Unclear objectives and priorities
- Lack of planning
- Stress and fatigue
- Inability to say no
- Desk management and personal disorganization

Of course, this list might not contain any problem areas for you. Perhaps you need to think through your own set of time stealers. Once you've identified the problem areas, then start to tackle them creatively. There are experts in the field of time management and books written on almost every one of the above-mentioned issues. If you are serious about taking control of your time, I encourage you to learn more.

I've identified a few of the most common hindrances to wise time management and have included some tips on incorporating good habits into your daily routine.

Follow Jesus's Approach to Dealing with Interruptions

Jesus says this about one kind of interruption: "And whoever welcomes a little child like this in my name welcomes me" (Matthew 18:5).

Interruptions are impossible to eliminate from our lives. In fact, since most interruptions involve people, I would contend that we don't want to abolish them entirely. I've learned that God does some of His best work through interruptions. It's often a test of our character as to how we respond. I learned this years ago when a friend made a simple comment.

"I know how busy you are, and I'm so sorry to bother you," she began. Her request was simple, and I was glad she asked. But afterwards I was pierced by her apology for "bothering" me.

Her comment haunted me. Why did she feel bad about asking for my help? Obviously I must give off the impression I'm too busy to be bothered. As I pondered this idea, God brought my own words to mind. I realized for many years, my standard answer to "How are you?" was, "I'm busy." If my friends couldn't tell how busy I was by watching my frantic schedule, then I felt obligated to tell them.

The kindness of my friend caused me to not only evaluate my oral language but also my body language and schedule. Did my words and lifestyle welcome the interruption of a friend in need, or put up a stop sign? I was sad to realize that a red light was flashing most of the time and my welcome mat was in storage.

I wondered how many opportunities to help a friend had been missed by my hectic life and don't-bother-me approach to interruptions. While I'd been checking items off my to-do list, had I missed something on God's to-do list?

Jesus definitely had a different approach to interruptions—He welcomed them. In Matthew 9, we read that Jesus was teaching His and John's disciples. I imagine them circled around Jesus, some on the ground, others on rocks, all leaning in to capture every word. In the middle of the lesson, a synagogue ruler named Jairus interrupted and asked Jesus to come help his sick daughter. The Scriptures record that Jesus got up and went with Jairus. Jesus didn't ask Jairus to come back later or sigh and reluctantly rise. The text implies that Jesus rose immediately and responded to the request for help.

People must have known that Jesus was approachable because this is just one of many instances where they interrupted Him. Jesus's demeanor must have welcomed hurting, scared, and lonely people to come when they felt the need. As Jesus responded with grace to the interruptions in His schedule, God worked miracles, and this time was no exception. But on this day, God worked two miracles.

Before Jesus could get to Jairus's daughter, a second interruption occurred. As Jesus walked through the crowded street, a woman reached out to touch His cloak. This woman, who had been bleeding for 12 years, was healed as she touched Jesus's garment. Jesus felt the healing power leave Him, and He stopped walking long enough to speak with the woman. After this interaction, Jesus continued His journey to Jairus's house, where He raised the daughter from the dead.

Two interruptions, two gracious and loving responses by Jesus, and two miracles. Imagine if Jesus had been too busy, or if Jairus or the woman had been afraid to bother Jesus. Imagine the ministry God might want to work through us when we welcome interruptions.

Jesus modeled a lifestyle of openness. Young and old, wealthy and poor, and healthy and sick all approached Him with questions and requests for help. Jesus's willingness to respond to the unexpected opened doors for God to work. Even though Jesus had a lot on His agenda, there was always time for a surprise need.

This is quite a different approach from most of the "expert" advice I've read on managing interruptions. I do believe there are times when we need to focus without interruptions. Perhaps it's not as often as we think. Because there will be times when we need to meet a deadline, here are some tips to balance our need to work with the interruptions that come our way.

Create "white space" in your day.
In other words, don't schedule every minute. If there really is no time for an interruption, then you are too busy.

Choose your words and tone of voice carefully.
When a friend or family member calls, express your delight to hear from them. If you can't talk, be honest and arrange to talk when it's more convenient. Friendships take time and effort to maintain, so schedule coffee or lunch with those people who matter most. In conversation, casually mention your work schedule, without

specifically saying, "Don't call then, please." A good friend will be listening and will take that into consideration.

Be direct.
If you have individuals in your life that don't honor your time, then a more direct approach will be needed. However, it can still be done with kindness. Of course, caller ID helps too because there's no law saying we always have to answer our phones.

Be thorough the first time.
Some interruptions are of our own making. If people contact you asking for more information on something you've prepared, perhaps you need to be more thorough the first time. Think through every question they might ask and even have someone else review your proposal, report, or letter before sending it. It's like sending out an invitation to a party without the date. You're going to get calls!

Pray About What Leadership Roles God Is Calling You to Do

Years ago I was asked to assume a leadership role at church. I was honored to be asked, and since I have the gift of administration, said yes without much thought or prayer. A few months into this new responsibility, it was evident I was in the wrong place. I was serving at a level where I learned too much about the inside workings of the church, about other leaders, and about members. It was a burden to carry all that information and I struggled with feelings of resentment, impatience, and anger. At that point in my life, I wasn't spiritually mature enough to be in that position of leadership, and there were pride issues that needed to be personally addressed. After one year, I resigned.

For that one year I served in a place I was not called to. I stepped into it without seeking the Lord's will and consequently was missing out on what God had really planned for me. Plus, I kept someone from fulfilling their calling by occupying their space.

I wonder how often that happens to others. There's an exciting and flattering opportunity presented. It sounds good and we accept the responsibility. Then we find ourselves overloaded and discouraged with all the associated tasks. Our attitudes sour and other areas of our lives are affected. These types of missed-calling responsibilities easily deplete our energy and enthusiasm.

Compare that to being exactly where God has called you. I know with certainty that God called me be home, and He opened me up to an entire world of serving Him through a national ministry. I'm still using my gifts of administration and leadership, but now I'm refreshed instead of drained.

If you dread an ongoing responsibility and feel discouraged instead of at peace, go to the Lord in prayer and seek His will. This could be an area that someone else is called to instead of you.

Overcome the Tendency to Procrastinate

The biggest thief of time in many of our lives is procrastination. The reasons for procrastination are varied. We feel overwhelmed with the task at hand, we're afraid, distracted, consumed with self-doubt, or are perfectionists. Regardless of our reasons for procrastinating, the results are often the same: increased stress, poor performance, and painful consequences. Bernard Meltzer said, "Hard work is often the easy work you did not do at the proper time."

Overcoming procrastination begins with identifying why we delay, then dealing with it on our own or getting help. We all procrastinate to some degree, so it's not anything to be embarrassed about. Perhaps these tips will help you:

1. Break up the task into manageable chunks.

Think through every action you'll need to take to accomplish the task. Write these down on 3-by-5 index cards. Then put the cards in the chronological order necessary to complete the assignment.

2. Set short-term goals with due dates.

These could be daily or even hourly, but assign a due date (or hour) to each step.

3. Reward yourself when you've met your due date.

This could be a walk around the block, reading a chapter of a novel, or a bubble bath. Create your own motivators throughout the project. When you're done, celebrate!

4. Just start.

When I teach writing workshops, I'm sometimes asked how to overcome writer's block. My answer seems simplistic even to me, but here it: Just start. Start at the beginning, the middle, or the end. It doesn't matter how good the product is, just start. That little piece of advice is freeing to many authors who think they've got to have it all together before turning on the computer.

Avoid Being Lured by the Internet or Email

The Internet offers an endless source of bunny trails. I think I'm focused on a research goal, when an interesting link presents itself at the end of an article. I click on it and find myself on the author's Web site, who recommends her favorite Web sites, and off I go. My curious mind is entranced by the lure of information available with a simple left click of the mouse. Thirty minutes later I drag myself back to the original task, only to find my mind left somewhere in cyberspace.

Dealing with this issue is a matter of focus and self-discipline. When you find yourself surfing the Internet, remind yourself what a waste of time it is. Bookmark those sites you'd like to review at a later date and get back on task.

Another time consumer is email, especially forwards. While some people simply delete forwards, I prefer to go directly to the sender with a kind request to remove me from their mailing lists. I start by thanking them for thinking of me, but explain that I'm trying to reduce the amount of emails I receive, and ask to be removed from their forwarding list. I've never had anyone get annoyed, and it sure reduces the temptation to read funny stories.

work @ home

Tackle Personal and Home Disorganization

When your company paid your salary and subsequently covered your wasted time, the two hours a day that you may have lost due to moderate disorganization was bad. Now that you're the boss, the money you lose as a result of wasted time comes out of your own pocket, and that's really bad.

In *12 Steps to Becoming a More Organized Woman*, Lane Jordan offers this reason to be organized:

Why should you be organized? Being organized will give you more time for the most important people in your life, your family. But beyond that, the Bible shows that God is a God of order. Order creates peace, calmness, and efficiency. God created one thing at a time, each on a specific day. He organized His creations until He was ready to create the best: us.

The rest of this chapter offers some very practical advice on how to organize different areas of your home. If being better organized can give you two more productive hours a day, it's worth spending some time on the practical side of life.

Capture Your Thoughts and Save Them for Review

The short-term memory part of our brain is only designed to hold just so much information. Author and productivity expert David Allen describes our mental limitations in his book *Getting Things Done*. He compares the part of our brain that holds all of the incomplete, undecided, and unorganized "stuff" to the RAM on a computer. Allen writes, "Most people walk around with their RAM bursting at the seams. They're constantly distracted, their focus disturbed by their own internal mental overload."

This problem translates into tension that's difficult to pinpoint. Allen continues, "As soon as you tell yourself that you need to do something, and store it in your RAM, there's a part of you that thinks you should be doing that something all the time. . . . Frankly, as soon as you have two things to do stored in your RAM, you've generated personal failure, because you can't do them both at the same time."

The answer is to capture the thoughts that run through your mind and deposit them in a safe place where you can review them at the appropriate time. This means always having a grocery list, an errand list, a to-do list, a someday-I'd-like-to list, and so on. If you have personal or professional goals, those should be written down and filed.

This is why a filing system is so important for your business and personal life. I've included tips on creating a filing system in chapter 14 if you'd like to review them.

Create a Correspondence Center

Staying in touch with friends, sending a get-well card, and paying bills are all necessary and thoughtful parts of our lives. Yet we can spend a lot of time running to the store for a birthday card or stamps because we've run out. Gather all that correspondence into one central location to save both time and money.

First, create a mailing center, whether it's in a desk drawer or accordion file. This file can contain your bills arranged by the date they need to be mailed, an assortment of greeting cards, and stamps. If remembering your loved ones' special events is important to you, sign and address cards once a month and put them in order with your bills so they get mailed on time. Buy a sufficient amount of stamps to avoid frequent trips to the post office.

Incoming correspondence takes a different response. To avoid overflowing piles of paper, missed deadlines, or opportunities, sort through your mail every day. Have a predesigned plan for dealing with every item.

- Purchase a shredder for all documents that contain any type of account number.
- Recycle unnecessary paper.
- Put bills in bill center. Write the mailing date on the corner and file in that order.
- File important documents, such as bank statements, in permanent file storage.
- RSVP immediately to invitations and special events, then

write important dates on the calendar.

- Put invitations and special event flyers containing pertinent information in a special file until the date of the event.
- For items that need your attention, put in a to-do basket in your work area.

Systematically Process Printed Material
Special Cards, Papers, and Letters

If you're like me, you love to hold on to birthday cards you've received, a love note from your spouse, or a drawing from a child. Those items hold precious memories for me, such as the self-portrait my eldest son did in kindergarten—it was a rainbow.

Instead of tossing them in big plastic tub, create some simple organization. An uncomplicated way to start is by filling a three-ring binder with acid-free plastic page protectors. Just date the item, slip it into a page protector and you're done.

To save my children's birthday cards, I put them in gallon resealable plastic bags. These bags are stored in memory boxes in each child's room. I also tuck the guest list and a list of gifts received into the bag, along with a description of the party.

Magazines

Magazines have a way of multiplying in my house. To conquer this source of clutter, have a plan and sequence for each magazine. When they arrive in the mail, place unread magazines in a specific holder. A great time-management tip is to carry reading material in a shoulder bag when you are out and about. While waiting, just pull out a magazine.

Once you're done reading the magazine, move to the next stage in its life. Store it in an attractive holder in your bookcase; clip and save interesting articles, while recycling the rest of the magazine; or pass it on to a friend, a doctor's waiting rooms, or a retirement community.

Phone Numbers, Addresses, and Passwords

Eliminate little pieces of paper! Let this be your organizing theme.

A wonderful tool that works for me is a Rolodex-type address box. That's the kind with the removable cards. My advice is to transfer every name, address, and phone number to this type of system. The beauty of this system is that you can discard numbers you no longer need without messing up an address book. This type of system can also be used to store low- to medium-risk Web site passwords and account numbers. However, for high-risk accounts, use a different password and store it in a different place.

Children's School Papers

With our first child we save everything! Unless you have lots of storage, this may get difficult as the years go on and as you have more children. To keep your kids and you organized, here are some tips that work for us.

1. Purchase a colored pocket folder for each child. Every year we get welcome letters from the teacher, classroom rules, student lists, and a school handbook. To keep that information handy, yet organized, I purchase an inexpensive colored pocket folder for each child. These folders lie flat in a kitchen drawer, ready for easy access.

2. Create another file for school items you want to save. In our permanent file drawers each child also has his or her own hanging file. Because it's not feasible to save everything, I have some criteria for what gets saved:
   - Something that shows my child's development at that age
   - Papers with teacher notes of praise
   - Papers that show an area of struggle
   - Something that shows my child's uniqueness, such as drawings, stories, and poems

3. At the end of the school year, purchase 9-by-12 see-through expandable plastic envelopes from an office supplies store. Most school papers fit inside this envelope. Put your child's school picture in the front, along with a piece of paper stating the school year. These can be easily stored in an under-the-bed box.

4. To help out-of-state grandparents or other family members

keep in touch with your child's development, consider sending some of the school papers and drawings to them. To ease the process, keep a 9-by-12 addressed envelope at the ready, and mail once a month. Another tip is to write a letter on the back of the drawings, making it into a homemade card.

Family Fun Book

Have you ever picked up a museum brochure or a take-out menu from your favorite restaurant and wondered where to put it? Consider creating your own Family Fun Book. This can be done with a three-ring binder with tabbed inserts. Set up different sections depending on your family's interests. As you collect information, either put it in plastic page protectors or three-hole punch it. Here are some potential categories:

- Restaurant menus
- Party ideas
- Museum/activity brochures
- Movies you want to see or rent
- Ideas for day trips
- Vacation ideas
- Decorating tips

There's a more important reason for better managing our time or organizing our homes than simply getting more done. I believe it comes back to the concept of stewardship. The Scriptures are clear: We will be asked to account for what we've been given: "Now it is required that those who have been given a trust must prove faithful" (1 Corinthians 4:2).

Even as I write these words of practical advice, I know there are beautiful brothers and sisters in Christ who struggle with this issue of time management. There are those who may read this chapter with discouragement because their counters are overflowing and they constantly lose things. Take heart. God does not want you to feel condemnation over this.

If this is an area that is weighing you down, I encourage you to confess it to some close friends and ask for advice and wisdom. I once had a friend share her disorganization with me in private. It was an embarrassment to her and was upsetting her husband. Within a few weeks, we had arranged a workday and even included another friend. With three of us sorting through papers and toys we were able to make a noticeable difference in just one day. It was just what my friend needed to jump-start her own work.

I believe that God has great plans for you and your time. With His help, you can create an orderly schedule and home.

CHAPTER 18
· · · · · · · · ·

MONEY-SAVING IDEAS

A penny saved is a penny earned."
I don't hear many folks repeating this time-worn saying of Benjamin Franklin's. Maybe people have forgotten that this is actually true.

Consider this question: Does saving $100 by frugal spending or earning $100 put more money in your pocket? If you earn $100, you will pay $10 for your tithe and about $15 on taxes. That leaves $75. But by saving $100, you actually have $100 to spend somewhere else. Plus, if you put that $100 into some sort of investment or savings account, it will be worth more over time.

When I was working full-time outside my home, my time was often worth more than saving a few dollars. When I started working at home, my income was reduced and saving money increased in importance. I learned quickly that I needed to approach my spending with a new attitude.

Saving money takes intentional thinking and advance

planning to do it effectively and make a noticeable difference in your budget. It's more than buying bland generic items or clipping coupons. Unfortunately, that's the first thing that enters many people's minds when they think of frugal living.

I find that saving money is more like an adventure. Because I'm a steward of God's money, it becomes a challenge to purchase the highest-quality item at the best price. I believe God wants me to care for my family's needs and have enough left over to share with others in need. If I have nothing left over, there's not much to share. Saving money allows me to be more generous in my giving.

There's a beautiful Scripture passage about generosity: "You will be made rich in every way so that you can be generous on every occasion, and through us your generosity will result in thanksgiving to God. This service that you perform is not only supplying the needs of God's people but is also overflowing in many expressions of thanks to God. Because of the service by which you have proved yourselves, men will praise God for the obedience that accompanies your confession of the gospel of Christ, and for your generosity in sharing with them and with everyone else" (2 Corinthians 9:11–13).

According to this Scripture passage, when we share what we have with those in need, that generosity will result in thanksgiving and praise to God. If our thriftiness leads to greater generosity and greater generosity leads to men and women praising God, then I say, "Bring on the coupons!"

My philosophy about spending money is simple: I can save money in every item on my budget with careful planning. That means the opportunities for saving are all around me. But where do you start if you've never thought much about saving? I suggest we start with the small stuff and expand from there.

Small Expenses

The easiest and quickest place to start saving is where you spend your cash, or any expense under $25. The next question is, can you save money by doing this yourself? This might involve making some equipment purchases, but the savings over time will compensate for the expense. Here are some suggestions to get you started:

School lunches. If your child purchases a hot lunch, the first step to savings is making her lunch. There are many ways to make a sack lunch appealing with creative entrée items. Consider buying a picnic cookbook for ideas. Investing in a wide-mouth thermos container for hot items breaks up the monotony. If your child already takes her lunch, look for ways to save by buying in bulk and dividing into serving portions. Fruit cocktail, chips, and cookies lend themselves to bulk buying.

Haircuts. Years ago I got tired of paying someone to cut my boys' and husband's hair. It didn't look that hard. A $25 purchase of clippers lasts about a year and saves us at least $50 every six weeks.

Snacks. Kids (and adults) get hungry at the most inopportune times. Even driving by a fast-food restaurant makes my kids hungry. To avoid overpriced packaged snacks, carry healthy food in a cooler in the car. If you know you'll be doing errands, put water bottles, fruit, or crackers in a cooler. This does two things. First it separates true hunger from bored eating. When someone says no to an apple, you can bet he or she isn't that hungry. Second, it makes healthy snacks easily accessible.

Dry cleaning. With the high cost of dry cleaning, this is an important expense to consider. Research if there is a discount dry cleaner in your area. This type of cleaning works on most items. Another option is to purchase a coupon book, like the *Entertainment Book*. There normally are 50 percent off dry cleaning coupons for every month of the year. Visit entertainment .com for information on buying a book.

Starbucks. This warrants mentioning as a high expense for many of us. I have to admit a fondness for Mocha Malt Frappuccino myself. It is possible to come close to the specialty coffee flavor at home. It may involve purchasing an espresso machine or a high-quality blender, but consider the money you can save.

Fast food. With the abundance of $1 menus, one would think fast food is cheap. Those cheap items are low-price leaders. Once you get in the restaurant, your bill quickly rises, not to mention your cholesterol. Fast food should be the exception, rather than the rule. However, when you do want an easy meal, consider buying everyone a $1 burger, and once home, throwing a bag of frozen french fries in the oven and serving it all with a fruit salad.

Medium Expenses

Once you've thoroughly considered the smallest expenses on your budget, work your way up to the next level. Take a look at those expenses in the $50 to $250 range. If you need to, go through your checkbook item by item and list your expenses.

Water. Not only is this a great budget area in which to save money, but it's ecologically important. Although most of these tips only save small amounts of water, over time the savings will add up.

- Landscaping. Make sure you aren't watering more than necessary. Try cutting back a minute or two each day. Plant low-water-use flowers and bushes.
- Water-saving devices. These can be installed on faucets, and most new toilets already have them. In toilets without this function, you can fill a one-quart plastic bottle with water and place it in the toilet tank to displace water. To anchor the bottle, partially fill it with sand or any heavy substance. This does not affect the efficiency of most toilets and can save five or more gallons per day per a family of four. Do not use bricks to displace water in your toilet tank. Bricks break down over time and can cause problems.
- Leaks. Fix promptly. Until you can fix them, collect the water and use it on your plants.
- Showers. All of us let some water go down the drain waiting for it to warm up. Consider collecting some of the cold water and using it on your plants.
- Leftover water or ice in glasses. Instead of pouring it down the drain, dump leftover water or ice into your houseplants.

Cable. Cut back on your package or eliminate altogether.

Telephone/Cell phone. My parents had one choice for phone service. Today we have no excuse for not shopping around. One thing I've learned is that your phone service provider will not call you when there's a lower priced package available to you. A check with my cell phone provider got me 50 more minutes a month for no extra charge. Speak with a customer service representative and let him or her know you are shopping and directly ask if the provider can offer you any discounts.

Gas. Try to coordinate your errands. Start a list of places you need to go and then set aside a block of time to make several stops at once. With the price of gas, who can afford to run out every day? This is also a time-management tip.

Clothing. The clothes my mother didn't make herself were purchased on sale from the nicer department stores. This afforded my sisters and me well-made clothing in last season's style.

- Used clothing stores in an upscale part of town are the source of many great bargains. That same area of town is often a good place to find yard sales with affordable clothes.
- Another way to save money on clothing is to arrange a clothing swap. Quite often friends are uncomfortable offering hand-me-downs. But if you let it be known you accept them and are willing to share your kid's clothes with others, you might just put together an ongoing clothing exchange.

Entertainment. To find affordable family activities, start thinking like a visitor to your city and state. Bookstores are filled with guidebooks with free and low-cost outings. I recommend you start a Family Fun Book as described in the previous chapter and collect information on free days at museums, hikes, and parks. If your city has any state or federally owned parks, inquire about the ranger program. One of our local mountain parks offers great free programs, including cooking with a dutch oven.

- National Park System—One of my family's best investments is the National Park Pass. For only $50 a year our entire family can enter any national historic site, park, or monument. When we travel, we check our guidebook and those are the first sites we visit. The ranger programs are always top-notch and noncommercial. One of our best memories was visiting Jamestown. Our visit started with an introduction and guided tour by a ranger dressed in historically accurate clothing and speaking as the inhabitants did in the 1500s. Not only is this an affordable family activity, but we sneak in a history lesson as well.

Large Expenses

Don't overlook your large budget expenses when trying to be cost conscious. You might be able to make the biggest impact in these areas.

Home utilities. There are many ways to save in this area because it's used all over our house. Energy-efficient choices can save a family up to 30 percent of their bill. Most local utility companies actually want you to conserve energy and will offer online advice for your specific geographic location. Here are some general tips for saving money on this monthly expense:

- Heating and cooling expenses account for 56 percent of our monthly utility bills, according to the US Department of Energy. Depending on your geographic location, switching to high-efficiency air conditioners and taking other actions to keep your home cool could reduce this energy use by 20 percent to 50 percent. Likewise, those living in colder climates should consider upgrading their furnace if their annual fuel utilization efficiency (AFUE) rating is low. Visit the US Department of Energy's "Energy Efficiency and Renewable Energy" Web site for a comprehensive savings evaluation based on the AFUE for your home (www.eere. energy.gov/consumer/your_home/).

- Make sure your home is properly weatherized to avoid loss of warm or cool air. Many utility companies either offer this energy audit service for free or can refer you to a specialist.

- Change air filters once a month to ease the strain on your heating and cooling equipment. If you have pets, you may need to replace the filters more often.

- Windows are the source of 50 percent of heat gain or loss. In hot climates, shading your full-sun windows can save up to 25 percent on your air-conditioning expense. In cold climates, draw the drapes to keep warmth in.

- Check the insulation in your attic. Those in the sunny southern parts of the country need insulation with an R rating of 19–30. Those in the beautiful North should make sure theirs has an R-49 value.
- Keep your freezer or refrigerator full, but not overcrowded. Use water or bags of ice to fill up empty space.
- During the summer, run the dishwasher and dryer during the coolest part of the day to reduce work on the air-conditioning. In winter, run those same appliances during the coolest part of the day to increase the warmth in the house.
- Allow dishes to air-dry in the dishwasher, saving up to 20 percent of that appliance's electricity cost by eliminating the heating function.
- Use slow cookers and outdoor grilling during the summer months. If you aren't well versed in these styles of cooking, purchase a cookbook or two. I figure if a cookbook saves me from going out for dinner one night, it's already paid for itself.
- Use your microwave oven when possible. Purchase a cookbook if you are unsure what will work in the microwave.
- Replace incandescent, or standard, light bulbs with compact fluorescent lights (CFLs). Although they cost more to purchase, they use 75 percent less energy and last up to ten times longer.
- Turn off lights when not in use, especially in the summer. The heat from the bulbs makes your air conditioner work harder.
- Approximately 90 percent of the energy used to wash clothes goes to heating water, so wash as many loads in cold water as possible.
- Dry consecutive loads to take advantage of the heat stored in your dryer.
- Take short showers instead of baths. A five-minute shower typically uses less than 10 gallons of water, while a bath uses 15–25 gallons.

- To prevent unnecessary heat loss, use lids on pots and pans on the stove.

Insurance. There's no replacement for shopping around for auto and homeowners insurance. Other ways to reduce your expenses are to raise your deductible.

Mortgage. If you haven't looked at your current mortgage interest rate lately, this might be an area to consider. If you do refinance, try and get the shortest repayment schedule you can afford. Remember your goal is to save money, not just lower your monthly bills.

Food. This is my favorite area in which to save money. I love to watch shows about food, read cookbooks, look at grocery ads, go shopping, and cook. As I try to creatively reduce my food budget, I find that my family actually eats healthier foods and enjoys the variety. Here are tips that work consistently in my home:

- Create a weekly menu. This is a must to save money on food. The best time to make your menu is when you are hungry. If you are full, nothing sounds good. Once you're hungry, set some time aside with the grocery store ads and cookbooks. If you don't own any, check out cookbooks with photos at the library. Then create your menu for the week. Remember to include side dishes, fruits, and vegetables. If you pull a recipe from a cookbook, make a written note on your menu of the book and page number.

- Shop sales. This isn't as hard as it sounds. We have saved so much money by planning our menu around what's on sale that week. I've found the Internet to be my best friend in this department. I am not very confident in cooking different cuts of beef. I've found I can take the name of a specific cut of meat on sale, type it into a search engine, and voilà, I've got a handful of ways to prepare dinner.

- Stock up on sales items. Inadequate storage is usually the reason this is a challenge. Perhaps you can convert some garage space for storage of nonperishable items.

- Use coupons. Even if you don't read the newspaper on a daily basis, pick up the Sunday paper or ask a friend for the coupon section. Coupons are also available online. Use your favorite search engine to track them down. Finally, the trick is to watch for sales and then use a coupon on top of that.

- Buy in bulk. Having five kids, buying in bulk is economical for us. If you find yourself wasting food purchased in bulk, consider shopping with a friend and dividing your purchases. Another option is to invest in freezer bags and divide and freeze potions for later.
- Discover outlet grocery stores and bakeries. A quick check through your yellow pages should reveal some outlet food stores. A bakery outlet down the street sells high-quality products at less than half the price of a grocery store. Freeze what you don't eat right away.

General Money Saving Tips

In addition to the specific tips listed in this chapter, I'd also like to share some general money-saving advice that has helped our family along the way.

Rent or borrow instead of buy. Renting isn't always the best advice, but it can work on some items. Instead of buying an item you'll use once a year, consider renting. Rent landscaping or construction tools, a steam cleaner, boat, skis, trailer, or an RV. In our neighborhood, we've saved money by doing our annual landscaping work on the same day and sharing the rental fee.

Make the library your friend. Check out recipe books, how-to books, best-sellers (get on the waiting list), and magazines. Not only do you save money by not buying these items, but you reduce clutter by not having to store them long-term.

Buy used. Who doesn't love the smell of a new car? As the aroma wears off, we're left with a vehicle that's losing 20 to 30 percent of its value in the first year and depreciating in value in subsequent years. That means the average new car sold in 2006 with a sticker price of over $28,000 lost about $8,400 in the first year.

The bad news doesn't stop there. That $28,000 car doesn't cost $28,000. Assuming a five-year payment period at 6.5 percent interest, that car actually costs $33,000. Throw in another $5,000 for taxes, licensing, and other fees, and you now have a $38,000 vehicle, which may have a residual value of $10,000 after five years. That car cost you $28,000 to drive for five years.

Another option is to buy a used car. Let's say you find a good car for $15,000. The best plan is to pay cash. If that's not possible, assume a 7.5 percent used car interest rate for three years and your cost is about $17,000. Add $3,000 for taxes, licensing, and other fees, and you're up to $20,000. The good news is the car has a residual value of $8,000. Subtract that value from the actual cost, and you've paid $12,000 to drive a used car for five years. That's a savings of $16,000 over the new car.

Now, take that $16,000 and invest it in a mutual fund over five years at a modest 6 percent rate of return and your savings are now almost $22,000.

There are challenges in buying a used car, so you need to do your homework. The Federal Trade Commission offers sound advice. Visit their Web site at www,ftc.gov and click on For Consumers. You'll find links containing advice for many different consumer purchases. *Consumer Report*'s Web site offers specific recommendations for used cars. Their site is www .consumerreports.org.

Plan in advance. Planning in advance saves you time and money. Life is pretty repetitive in some areas. Children outgrow their clothes, people celebrate birthdays, and most of us take vacations. For those expenses that are infrequent but dependable, try planning ahead.

- Clothing. At summer's and winter's end, take a clothing assessment for each family member. Give away or save for a yard sale those items that are outgrown or are no longer your styles. Then, make a shopping list of what you know you'll need for the next year's season and start watching sales, consignment stores or other people's yard sales.
- Gifts. One summer we vacationed near a Legos outlet store. With three boys under 12 years of age, I was always buying Legos for birthday gifts. The prices were too good to pass up and I stocked up. The inexpensive Legos got tucked in my birthday box along with other bargains picked up throughout the year. For family gifts, try and have a specific

individual in mind when making a purchase. I keep a gift journal to remember what I've bought for whom.

- Travel. Vacation plans can blow your budget if you aren't careful. There are bargains available for those willing to search. Consider joining the American Automobile Association to get discounts on travel, lodging, and dining. The *Entertainment Guide* is a fantastic source of discounts, especially in lodging. In most cities, there are partner hotels that offer a 50 percent discount from the rack rate. Most travel guides, like *Frommer's,* offer recommendations for free or inexpensive high-quality activities and food. Finally, we save money by making our own breakfast and one meal. Eating cereal out of the individual serving boxes is a treat for the kids and they never know we're being thrifty. We also enjoy finding a farmer's market and getting locally created artisan breads, cheeses, and meat for an impromptu picnic.

Evaluate savings opportunities over time. My family eats two loaves of 12-grain bread a week. I used to buy it at the grocery store and was willing to pay $3 a loaf for the quality. Then I learned my local warehouse store sold a pack of two loaves of a comparable brand of 12-grain bread for $4. If I bought nothing else at that store but bread, I would save $67 a year after the cost of membership. When I think about how savings on just one item can add up over the span of a year, I'm inspired to press on saving money.

Set money-saving goals. If you are a person who enjoys a challenge, set a money-saving goal for yourself. You might set a specific dollar amount, like saving $50 on your grocery bills. Perhaps you might set a percentage goal, say 5 percent on your electricity bill. Goals work because they allow us to measure our success and have something to celebrate . . . however, not by splurging on a fancy dinner!

Develop a repertoire of resources. There are many good books, magazines, and Web sites dedicated to saving money. For a flow of new ideas and encouragement, create a repertoire of resources. I'm always hesitant to recommend specific Web sites because I can't be 100 percent positive that every recommendation is biblically sound. Please do your own research with an eye to godly advice.

Wise spending is an important component of becoming a responsible financial steward. It's important to remember we should never be thrifty at the expense of another's welfare. I read an article from an author whose parents ran a restaurant. Occasionally, a hardworking waitress or waiter received a Christian tract instead of a tip. I'll give the restaurant guest the benefit of the doubt, but perhaps the tract could have been included along with a tip.

We are to have a generous, open-handed approach to all of the gifts God gives. I believe we should extend the money God has entrusted to us by ethically saving on expenses when possible and spending generously when called to do so.

CHAPTER 19
. . . .

SIX WAYS TO OVERCOME DISCOURAGEMENT

The joys of working at home far outweigh the difficulties. But difficulties have a way of sidelining even the stoutest heart. This chapter is for those days when you want to throw in the towel.

"Therefore, since we are surrounded by such a great cloud of witnesses, let us throw off everything that hinders and the sin that so easily entangles, and let us run with perseverance the race marked out for us" (Hebrews 12:1).

Decide in Advance Not to Quit

A few years ago, my husband ran his first marathon in Vancouver, Canada. Seeing as how I can't run around the block without having to go to the bathroom, I was very proud of my beloved and quite impressed with his accomplishment.

Tod's preparation for the race was grueling and organized. He first read a book on marathon running and mapped out his five-month training plan using a spreadsheet. Every week he increased his running distance until he was ready for the big day.

I'm happy to report that he finished the race within minutes of his expected time. To say that after all that planning and training the race was easy would be giving the wrong impression. At mile 23, when the "evil" race planners (at least that's what Tod called them) took the route up a hill, my husband felt like quitting. It took every ounce of commitment and energy to finish that race. But finish he did.

Working at home is like running a marathon, and it can be grueling at times. We think we've prepared and trained enough, but when our bodies and emotions are drained, when finances are tough, when it's so-o-o-o much harder than we thought, we can feel like quitting. There will be times when you think, "This is too much—I can't go on."

God knows how difficult life is. He knows what our personal race route looks like. He knows where we have hills that seem too difficult to climb. Knowing we will face difficulties, how can we run this life with endurance and continue in our home-based work when it gets tough?

One of the best ways to persevere is to decide in advance that you won't quit when things get tough. My husband determined that he would finish the race before he ever left the starting line. Quitting wasn't an option—even when his legs were aching, his lungs were burning, and he was surprised by a hill.

When you decide in advance that you will stay true to your calling to work at home, you can face the difficult days and the times when God seems distant. When you choose in advance to trust God even when you can't explain your circumstances, your faith grows. It is awesome when you come through a challenge and can look back and see how God worked through it all.

Set your eyes on heaven and trust God's goodness. When you face your personal hill, you'll see it as a stairway to greater intimacy with God, instead of a reason to quit the race.

"Carry each other's burdens, and in this way you will fulfill the law of Christ" (Galatians 6:2).

Surround Yourself with Cheerleaders

In addition to our perseverance, the support of others can help us continue during difficult times. As I learned at my first marathon experience, cheerleaders on the sidelines are an important part of the success of any race.

After I had given Tod a final hug and he joined the thousands of people leaving the starting line, I started walking back to the hotel. As I walked through the streets of downtown Vancouver, I realized I was walking along the race route. Spectators lined the streets and excited families clustered, waiting for a glimpse of their loved one. As I joined a small group of people on a corner, a uniformed volunteer told me the race leaders would be along any minute. Seeing that the race had started only 30 minutes before, I figured my husband would be right behind the leaders. So I determined to wait and surprise him.

While waiting for the racers, I overheard one family discussing their marathoner, who would be among the leaders. Their eyes scanned the distance waiting for the front-runners to appear. When they saw their guy, this little group yelled his name, shouting words of encouragement. Within seconds after he turned the corner, they set off, race map in hand, to get to the next spot where they would once more cheer him on.

I can only imagine how important his family's encouragement was to that runner. What a difference a positive word makes when we face personal challenges. Knowing that even one person believes in us can sustain us when we feel like giving up. The writer of Hebrews knew we would need each other to run with endurance. In Hebrews 10:25, he advised the early believers to "not give up meeting together, as some are in the habit of doing, but let us encourage one another."

The encouragement of others is integral to sustaining energy and focus. Plan to get involved in a support group of some kind. It could be a Bible study or a group of friends who also work at home. Stay faithful in your church attendance and develop godly friendships. Ask God to bring a friend with the gift of encouragement.

"Therefore, my beloved, be steadfast, immovable, always excelling in the work of the Lord, because you know that in the Lord your labor is not in vain" (1 Corinthians 15:58 NRSV).

Be Clear About Your Purpose

Occasionally I go through unproductive periods of time. When that happens, I know I lack focus. There's so much that I want to do I'm often scatterbrained. I allow myself to be pulled in multiple directions, intrigued by the possibilities of a new and exciting project. Staying focused and purposeful requires discipline that doesn't come naturally to me.

Jesus, on the other hand, is a picture of discipline. We learn much about His character in John 4. Here we find the story of Jesus meeting a woman at a well in Samaria. The disciples had gone to find something to eat while Jesus rested by a well. It was the middle of the day, the outside temperature was warm, and Jesus was weary and thirsty from the journey. Despite His physical discomfort, Jesus focused on the eternal needs of a woman who was living a life far from God.

The disciples returned with food and wanted Jesus to eat. "'My food,' said Jesus, 'is to do the will of him who sent me and to finish his work'" (John 4:34).

Jesus knew His purpose. He knew what His Father had asked Him to do and was committed to finish the work, in spite of the circumstances. In this passage, Jesus modeled clarity of purpose, perseverance, and compassion, all characteristics that are necessary if we are to finish the task God has called us to.

If God has called you to work at home, by doing so you are being obedient. An obedient life is defined by discipline. It takes discipline to obey God when we want to quit. It takes discipline to finish what we start. It takes discipline to stay focused on a difficult task instead of being distracted by a more enjoyable activity. Discipline and purpose often require sacrificing comfort and pleasure.

If you feel like you are always starting things and never finishing or are lacking focus, perhaps you need to pare down the activities in your life and focus on one or two things that God is calling you to do today. In *The Purpose-Driven Life,* Rick Warren says, "You have just enough time to do God's will."

When you feel overwhelmed, don't try to tackle everything at once. Ask God for His priorities for this one day, then concentrate on doing your best in those areas.

"Be strong and courageous. Do not be terrified; do not be discouraged, for the Lord your God will be with you wherever you go" (Joshua 1:9).

Step Out in Faith

Obedience to God's calling on my life is seldom easy. As I've sought to obey God over the years, I find I'm often out of my comfort zone. This seems to be a common denominator among those who radically obey God. They must step out in faith, risking discomfort, rejection, and failure.

I know this from personal experience and from watching others obey God, yet I still ask why. Why do I have to get out of my comfort zone? Why can't I serve God from the comfort of my recliner? Why can't this just be easy?

I've found three reasons:

1. If obedience is something we can easily do, we can take the credit and the glory. On the other hand, stepping out of our comfort zone requires us to rely on God. Then when the task is accomplished, we give God all the glory.

2. One of God's most effective ways to grow our faith is to stretch it. We don't learn to trust God by reading a book or listening to a great sermon. We don't learn to trust God by hearing how our friend trusts God. We learn to trust God by living out a real-life adventure with God and discovering for ourselves that He is trustworthy. You see, when you do something you never thought you could do, you see God's hand in the smallest of details. You forgive someone you never thought you would and you experience a peace you have never known. You step off a cliff and God provides an

invisible bridge. You tithe when you don't know how you'll do it, and God covers your needs. Then you learn: God can be trusted.

3. We find God on the other side of our comfort zone. God is too big and has too much to do to be limited by our insecurities. We are in a battle of eternal importance and it's not in God's nature to seek comfort. So if we want to go where God is, we need to step out on faith.

God is bold, not timid. God is brave, not afraid. God sees things in light of eternity. We see things in light of the moment. God is everything we aren't, but want to be.

John Ortberg has written a book entitled *If You Want to Walk on Water, You've Got to Get Out of the Boat.* The entire book is about the account in Matthew 14 of Jesus calling Peter to get out of the boat and walk on water.

You probably know the story. One evening, Jesus fed 5,000 men, plus women and children, with five loaves of bread and two fish. Immediately after that, He told the disciples to get in a boat and go on ahead of Him. Jesus dismissed the people and went to pray. It was the middle of the night and the disciples were already a distance across the water when Jesus decided to take a midnight stroll across the lake.

When the disciples saw Jesus approaching the boat, they were afraid. The disciples were terrified at the very thought of someone walking on water. But Jesus reassured them that He was approaching. Peter didn't believe Him and said: "Lord, if it's you, tell me to come to you on the water." Jesus replied, "Come."

I've thought a lot about this passage and have one question: Why does Peter tell Jesus to invite him to walk on the water? That's just asking for trouble in my book. Why didn't Peter just say, "If it's really You, Jesus, then what's Your mother's maiden name?"

Here's what John Ortberg says about Peter's question: "I believe there are many good reasons to get out of the boat. But there is one that trumps them all: The water is where Jesus is. The water may be dark, wet, and dangerous. But Jesus is not in the boat."

Peter wanted to be with Jesus, and was willing to do

whatever it took—including getting out of the boat. Today, Jesus is calling many of you out of your comfort zone through working at home. If you've never done this before, it will be scary and uncomfortable at times. But remember, Jesus never took the easy road. If we want to be with Jesus, we will need to step out in faith.

Deal Honestly with Your Fears

I hate being afraid. Of all the emotions, to me, fear is the worst. I feel completely helpless to protect myself, and I don't like being out of control.

Statistics don't help. It has been said that a large majority of things we fear never happen. Unfortunately, if 99 percent of the time something won't happen, I figure I'm in the 1 percent minority!

Positive self-talk doesn't help me. Try as I might, when I'm afraid, it does no good to just tell myself to not be afraid. The more I say, "I won't be afraid," the more my stomach knots and my heart pounds.

The disciples of Jesus had a better plan than trusting statistics or repeating positive phrases when they were afraid. They went right to the One who could address their fears.

While the disciples and Jesus were on a boat in the middle of a lake, a strong storm suddenly developed. In fact, it was so furious, the disciples were certain they would die. The Bible tells us they woke up Jesus, crying, "Lord, save us! We're going to drown."

Jesus responded to them saying, "You of little faith, why are you so afraid?" Matthew 8:26 tells us Jesus got up, rebuked the winds and waves, and the storm immediately calmed.

This story illustrates three actions we can take when we are afraid.

1. Admit we need Jesus to save us. Fear only increases when we hold onto the belief that we can save ourselves. Deep down, we know some things are completely out of our control. But nothing is out of Jesus's control.

2. Openly admit your fear. The disciples didn't say they were

afraid of the storm or of the boat being damaged. They admitted they were afraid of dying. Admitting our true fear often takes humility. But God desires honesty and can bring healing more easily to a humble heart.

3. Be in awe of Jesus. After Jesus calmed the storm, the disciples were "amazed." When God saves you from the source of your fears, honor Him for the miracle. Don't write it off as happenstance.

God proves Himself faithful to save us every day. We need to see with eyes like those of the first disciples and be amazed at what our God can do and has done. Jesus is still available to calm the winds and waves in your life today. What a mighty God we serve that even nature obeys Him!

"We wait in hope for the LORD; he is our help and our shield. In him our hearts rejoice, for we trust in his holy name" (Psalm 33:20–21).

Wait on the Lord

I told my first-grade son, Robbie, that I would bring him a special treat for lunch one day. He was overjoyed. He knew that several times a month for the past few years, I had been joining his older brothers for lunch at school and now it was his turn. He got to pick his favorite fast-food meal and sit at a special table with Mom.

I left the house with just enough time to pick up the food, but didn't anticipate a short-staffed restaurant. I waited my turn as the minutes ticked by, anxiously checking my watch every 30 seconds. If I could have jumped behind the counter to help, I would have.

The school schedule is exact, so I knew when Robbie would be walking from his classroom to the cafeteria. I knew when he would be sitting at a table, staring at the door, willing me to walk through it. Unfortunately, at that minute I was still in line.

I could have cried knowing my little boy was waiting and wondering where I was. Was I coming? Did I forget? Did something happen to me? Should he try and eat something from the cafeteria? "Hang on, Robbie," I thought. "I'm coming as fast as I can."

Finally, I got to the school about five minutes late, which is an eternity for a six-year-old. I raced into the cafeteria to find him sitting alone, with his little arms crossed on the table, and his head resting on his forearms. As I called his name, he looked up and his big brown eyes shimmered with unshed tears. But that quickly changed to joy when he saw the fast-food meal bag (oh, and me, of course).

I wish I could have erased the anguish Robbie felt during that wait. God must feel that same way as He watches His children wait on Him.

Although God's delays are never because of poor planning, sometimes we must wait upon His perfect timing. He knows He's just around the corner, with something even better than the fast-food meal we've asked for. He knows we often wring our hands, wondering if this time He'll forget. But the truth is, He never forgets. He watches us and knows our anxious thoughts. Although I couldn't comfort my son when I was delayed, God has sent the Holy Spirit to be our Comforter.

Waiting is never easy. The good news is, when we wait on the Lord, we can trust that it will be worth the wait. We need to rest in the knowledge that He never forgets, He never is late, and His plans for us will surpass even our greatest hopes.

At some point in your work-at-home journey, you may wonder where God is. You might wonder why He hasn't solved a problem, or why He's allowed something bad to happen. When your work at home isn't going according to your plans, you may be tempted to think you misheard God. When that happens, don't give up. Hang on and anticipate with joy how God is going to answer your prayers.

New Hope® Publishers is a division of WMU®, an international organization that challenges Christian believers to understand and be radically involved in God's mission. For more information about WMU, go to www.wmu.com. More information about New Hope books may be found at www. newhopepublishers.com. New Hope books may be purchased at your local bookstore.

OTHF
YOU ♦ ENJOY

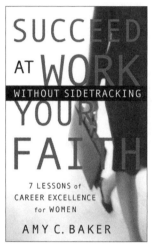

**Succeed at Work Without
Sidetracking Your Faith**
*7 Lessons of Career
Excellence for Women*
Amy C. Baker
1-56309-963-2

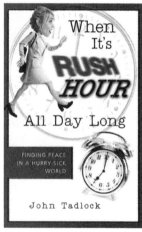

**When It's Rush Hour
All Day Long**
*Finding Peace in a
Hurry-Sick World*
John Tadlock
1-56309-770-2

**5 Leadership Essentials
for Women**
*Developing Your Ability
to Make Things Happen*
Compiled by Linda Clark
1-56309-842-3

Available in bookstores everywhere

For information about these books or any New Hope product, visit www.newhopepublishers.com.